The Fantasy Skirmish Game

Your Warband, Your Story

CONTENTS

Vanguard Game Design
Matt Gilbert with Ciaran Morris and
Andrew Sharp

Additional Development
Rob Burman, Stewart Gibbs

Painting
Dave Nield

Graphic Design
Duncan Aldis, Ben Sandum

Photography
Ben Sandum

Scenery
Tabletop World & the author's collection

Special Thanks

Simon Brown, Steven Clark, Vane
Dolenc, Tom Farley, Elvis Fisher, Rob
Harper, Matt Hobday, Kev Honeysett,
Marc Langworthy, Richard McAdam,
Calum McIntosh, Martin Penneck,
Philip Scicluna, Dave Symonds,
Rob Taylor, Donn Turner, Sharad Vora,
Alex Younger, and all our Kickstarter
Backers.

"Up! Up! Into them now!"

Hezketh roared his men on, letting the raw aggression of his voice give them courage and spur them forward into the melee.

The enemy had them. There was no point in deceiving himself, and it was on his head. He cursed himself for allowing them to be taken unawares in such a simple ambush. Another shower of arrows dropped among them and he saw someone on his left snatched back with a smack and a sudden intake of breath. They were tired, at the end of their endurance, a ragged remnant of the patrol that had set out to determine the enemy's strength. They had let their guard down, and now they were paying the price.

"Into them!"

His boots slipped and slid in the mud as he sought desperately to close the distance to the sudden enemy. His heart crashed against his ribs and an inchoate growl formed as he charged onwards, reverberating in his chest. He let the anger at his complacency feed his building rage, and the first flecks of white spittle began to speckle his beard.

The enemy were few but well armed, and Janah Hezketh knew well how vital it was that they escape this ambush as quickly as possible. He had seen too many patrols set upon and cut to pieces by ambushing archers, pinned down and then crushed by the oncoming infantry. He had fought in - even commanded - such attacks, and knew the lethal toll that could be levied upon a trapped and unsuspecting enemy once they were transfixed and afraid.

No, the secret was to break out, and to do it quickly. To his right Ralat and Jeneth kept pace with him. Ralat stayed close to Jeneth as he had told him to. The lad could learn from old Jeneth. It was for that reason he had put them together. He would learn, or he would die. Such was the way of things.

He gulped down air as mud gave way to earth and thin grasses. An arrow flashed past his face, black fletching making a dark smear across his vision for a fraction of a moment. Behind and to his left an answering shaft, then a second, sprang out into the brush that concealed the as yet unseen enemy. Morna and Sholen had strung their bows and were bringing them to bear on the foe. A sharp, brittle, scream of pain answered them and, in spite of the extremity of their plight, Hezketh found himself hoping that their few archers would not rob his axe of the chance to win him some glory.

The enemy were slight creatures, and seemed delicate, but this belied a wiry strength and a speed and agility that seemed scarcely possible. As he crested the rise, one stood to face him, spear raised. He brought back his axe in a wide arc and leapt.

"See me! See me and die!" The battle rage was upon him now, all reason and circumspection fled as he led Ralet and Jeneth crashing and screaming into the first of the enemy.

—•—

Hezketh sat on the fresh, steaming corpse of a horse that the enemy had clearly thought to ride away on after they had mopped up his little patrol. He looked up as Ralet approached. A bright splash of blood, red and vibrant, stained his young face and his eyes were alive with the joy of battle. "Janah, are you injured?" asked Ralet. Once, he supposed, he must have looked the same to the veterans of his company. Now, as the adrenaline ebbed away, he just felt tired.

"No lad," he answered, smiling at the young warrior. "Just tired from doing all the work for the likes of you, that's all." Just old. Just too old for this, he thought.

They had escaped. They had not deserved to.

"Jeneth?" he asked. Ralet could not meet his gaze. He just shook his head.

Janah closed his eyes. Friends would be left behind. And it was his fault.

WELCOME TO THE VANGUARD

Vanguard is the fantasy skirmish game set in the world of Mantica. It is a magical place, full of wonder, but also one of conflict and war, as almighty armies clash and empires crumble. Gods and demons roam the world and the skies light up with the crackle of magic. The mortal races strive for dominance across the vastness of the world; from the depths of the oceans, across to the deserts and plains, to the soaring mountain ranges and ice-covered peaks – there is adventure, glory and peril to be had in equal measure.

Vanguard gives you the chance to explore the world through the eyes of an elite Warband. As neighbours and kingdoms wage war, it's often the deeds of a hand-picked few - specialists in their trade - that ultimately win wars for their masters. Whether they are tasked with plundering an enemy camp, burning their stores, stealing information or assassination of an enemy commander, the scouting parties of the vanguard are always in the thick of the action, operating alone and in the greatest of danger.

Vanguard is a miniatures game, played on your tabletop, and puts you right at the heart of the action. In this book, you will find all the rules you need to play, ideas on how to paint your models and build amazing gaming tables, and also a detailed campaign system allowing you to develop your warband through a series of linked games with friends.

Can you guide your band of warriors to complete their missions and find fame and glory? Only time, skill and a little luck will tell.

Welcome to the Vanguard!

WHAT YOU WILL NEED

Models

Mantic Games supply a range of ready-made Warbands for Vanguard so it's easy to start your collection and get playing. You don't have to paint your models to play the game, but painting is a fantastic part of the gaming hobby and we would encourage you to do so. Playing with amazing looking miniatures you have painted yourself only adds to the fun!

Throughout this book, you will find wonderful examples of painted models and warbands to inspire your own collection.

The models for Vanguard are the same scale as the models used in Mantic's mass-battle game, Kings of War. Indeed, players of both games could easily use their Vanguard models as heroes and unit champions in their Kings of War armies.

Bases

Models should be glued to the square or rectangular base they are supplied with which will be the size appropriate for the model. A model, or parts of one, may extend over the base, but the base itself defines where the model is for all game purposes (such as measuring movement or range to a target).

Typically, human-sized models come on square 20mm or 25mm bases. Big brutes like ogres and trolls can be on 40mm or 50mm bases and cavalry models or similar will be on rectangular 25mm x 50mm bases.

Models should be positioned on their base in a way which clearly shows the way the model is facing so that it is obvious where the model's front and rear arcs are (see page 25).

Table and Terrain

You will need a firm, level playing surface to play your games of Vanguard. An area 3' x 3' is the standard size of playing space required, although it's possible to play on larger surfaces too.

Many players will build a collection of detailed terrain like hills, buildings, walls and trees which all adds to the realism of the game. If you don't already have a terrain collection however, you can simply use what you have to hand such as books and boxes.

Tape Measure

Distances and ranges in Vanguard are measured in inches.

Pre-measuring is allowed – you can check distances and ranges at any time during the game. When measuring to or from a model, use the model's base.

Dice

Vanguard uses two types of dice.

D8

8-sided dice are used for determining most actions and results in the game. These are rolled and read just like normal 6-sided dice.

You may sometimes have to roll more than one die to see what happens. For example, 2D8 means roll 2 8-sided dice and check each score.

Dice results may be modified. For example, a modifier of -1 means subtract 1 from each of your results. Unless specified otherwise, these are cumulative (e.g. two different +1 modifiers results in a +2 modifier for the roll).

Sometimes rolls may benefit from bonus dice (or even lose dice). Add or remove the number of dice specified before making the roll.

Power Dice

Power Dice are 6-sided dice with special symbols on them. They are rolled to generate Power which is then spent on Special Abilities and activations for your models in the game.

If the rules specify to roll a die, a D8 is implied. The rules will be explicit if a Power Die is to be used.

Re-rolls

Sometimes you will get the opportunity to re-roll one or more dice. You must accept the second result, even if it is worse than the first. You cannot re-roll an already re-rolled die!

Counters

Vanguard uses a number of counters to represent the status of models during play. These are placed next to the models as a reminder. Some have more than one status on them to help keep the number of counters on the table to a minimum. These are available to purchase separately.

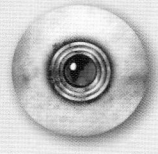 **Activated**

Braced

 **Fatigued**

Knocked-down

 **Wounds**

Spell Effects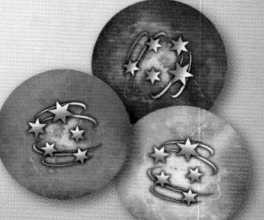

Model Stats

Not all Warbands and their warriors are equal. They will all have different abilities, strengths and weaknesses. In the game, these are represented by each model having a number of statistics (stats for short), skills, special rules and other game values. Warband stat cards are available as a great reference to use during the game so the details of your warband are easily at hand.

Each model in the Warband will have the following stats:

Faction Symbol

Which faction the model is fighting for. For example, Goblins, Northern Alliance, Basileans, Nightstalkers etc. Your Warband has a single faction, although it is possible to draft in other soldiers, such as Mercenaries.

Race

What race the model is. The model's Race is also a keyword that may interact with other rules.

Class

Models will be one (or more) of the following classes:

GRUNT, WARRIOR, SUPPORT, COMMAND, SPELLCASTER, LARGE

Class is important when building a Warband. A model's Class is also a keyword that may interact with other rules.

Height (H)

The height of a model affects how it interacts with other models and terrain for Line of Sight (LOS).

Speed (Sp)

This value shows the distance the model can move in inches.

Ranged (Ra)

This value is the target number the model needs to roll to hit a target when using a ranged attack, typically as part of a *Shoot* or *Cast* action.

Melee (Me)

This value is the target number the model needs to roll to hit an opponent when making a *Melee* attack.

Armour (Ar)

This value is the target number a model needs to roll to avoid taking damage and suffering wounds.

Nerve (Ne)

This value is the target number for any Nerve tests the model needs to take. This will come into play if the Warband is broken or if something unnerving happens!

Wounds (Wn)

This value shows the number of wounds the model can suffer before it is usually removed from play as a casualty. The larger the number, the more resilient (or stupid!) the model is.

Wound counters are used to track how many wounds a model has suffered. They are placed next to the model as each wound is suffered. When a model reaches 0 wounds (or fewer!), it is usually removed from the game as a casualty (too injured to continue...or possibly dead!).

Base

Each model's card or entry will indicate the model's base size (e.g. 20mm, 40mm etc.) A base size of **Cav** means a 25mm x 50mm cavalry base.

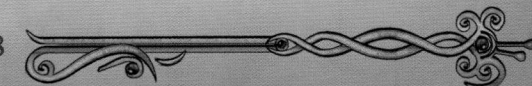

Equipment

Every model in the game is assumed to be naturally equipped with the basic weapons (or teeth, claws etc.) and armour they need to survive. However, some models come equipped with extra ranged weapons, specialist armour and even rare or magical artefacts. This will be listed on a model's stat card. Additional equipment can also be purchased for models (see page 120)

Attack dice

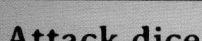

By default, models will use the number of Ranged or Melee attack dice stated on their stat cards. However, some equipment comes with its own replacement number of attack dice.

If the Type of equipment is followed by a number of dice, use that many dice (with any appropriate modifiers) when making an attack with the equipment.

For example, a Bow has a Type of Ranged. The model making a Ranged attack with a Bow uses the number of dice stated on its model stat card.

However, if the same model was given a Dwarf Flame Thrower, that equipment has a Type listed as Ranged (4D8). When the model uses the Flame Thrower to make a Ranged Attack, 4D8 would be used instead.

A model must have a weapon or spell with a listed range in order to make a Ranged Attack. If not, even if a number of dice are listed for the model, an attack cannot be made.

Equipment Cards

Some equipment may be represented using Vanguard equipment cards. If a card is used to represent a model's piece of equipment, it should be placed with the model's stat card as a reference during play.

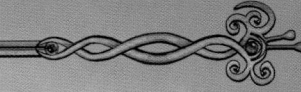

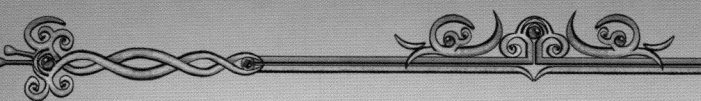

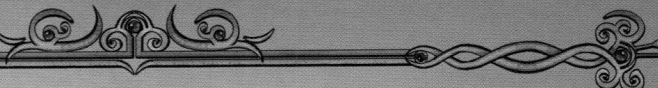

THE RULES

In a game of Vanguard, both you and your opponent take control of a Warband that you will be using to play an exciting skirmish encounter using your models. In each game, you will play a particular scenario that describes what each player needs to do to win. Maybe one side has to defend their army's baggage train from the enemy force, or perhaps both are fighting over control of a vital river crossing.

Once the battlefield has been set up with terrain and any objectives, the scenario you are playing will also tell you how to deploy your models ready to play. Details on how to set up the table ready for play are found on page 47.

The following pages are intended to introduce you to the rules in a prescribed way as follows:

- **The structure of the game**
  - Rounds and Turns
  - Rolling for Power
  - The End Phase
- **Things you can do**
  - Activations (and Actions)
  - Fatigue
  - Using Power
- **How you do them**
  - Movement
  - Arcs and Line of Sight
  - Ranged Attacks
  - Melee Attacks
  - Nerve

Exploding 8s!

For certain rolls in the game, a mechanism called Exploding 8s! is used.

This means that for each **natural** dice result of 8 in the roll (regardless of any modifiers), an automatic success is achieved and another bonus die can be rolled to see if a further success is achieved. It's possible to keep rolling 8s and to keep getting bonus dice!

Conversely, all **natural** die results of 1 (regardless of any modifiers) are automatic failures.

Scoring a 1 or an 8 after the application of any modifiers is not an automatic result.

Friendly Models

If a rule refers to friendly models, this means all models in your Warband.

Enemy Models

Conversely, your Warband's opponents are considered the enemy models in the rules.

Neutral Models

If a scenario requires other, third party models to be involved, these are considered Neutral.

Rounds and Turns

A game of Vanguard is played across a number of **Rounds**. Within each Round, players alternate taking **Turns**, activating their models, until both players have completed activating their whole Warband. A game might last a set number of Rounds, or be determined by a particular victory (or defeat!) condition. The scenario being played will tell you how long to play for. Typically, games last around 5 or 6 Rounds.

Game Sequence

1. Set up
2. Deploy your models
3. Determine who takes the first turn
4. Play Rounds
   a. Roll for Power
   b. Take alternating Turns, activating models
   c. End Phase
5. Determine the winner!

Who goes first?

The scenario being played will determine which side will take the first Turn in the first Round.

In subsequent Rounds, the player that finished activating their models first in the previous Round takes the **first** Turn in the new Round.

A Round will always begin with both players **Rolling for Power**. Players then take their alternating Turns. During each of their Turns, a player gets to do something (act) with a single model, or group of models, of their choice. Each model in a Warband only gets to act once in each Round. During the Turn in which it is acting, a model is known as the acting (or active) model. Once it has finished acting, the model is marked as **Activated** by placing an Activation counter next to it.

Taking Turns

Once a player has finished activating all their models and declares they are finished, the player with models yet to activate continues playing Turns until their models are also all Activated. Once a player has declared they are finished for the Round (including any/all Forced Fatigue Actions – see pages 19 and 20), they cannot then change their mind! All models must be Activated, even if they then don't perform any actions. Players may not choose to pass a Turn.

Once all models on both sides have Activated, no more Turns are played and the Round concludes with the **End Phase**.

Rolling for Power

Power Dice are a representation of the training, co-ordination and cunning of a well led and experienced fighting team. They are a limited resource that can be spent on accessing certain abilities or even boosting spells and attacks. Learning to manage your Power resource and when to spend it is a skill you will have to master!

1) Roll

At the start of each Round, before any Turns are taken, each player rolls their Power Dice. Create your pool of Power Dice by taking three RED Power Dice and then adding any extra dice as indicated on your Warband's stat cards (count only models that are still in play, not any removed as a casualty). These extra dice will be either RED, WHITE or BLUE. Roll all your Power Dice simultaneously.

2) Re-Roll

After rolling, starting with the player who will go first this Round, both players may re-roll one of their Power Dice for each model of COMMAND Class they have on the table in play. If a player re-rolls any of their dice, they must keep the new result(s).

Important: If no models with the COMMAND Class are left alive in a Warband, that player loses the ability to re-roll any Power Dice.

3) Set

Finally, each player sets their Power Dice results beside their edge of the table. They will be available to spend on augmenting the actions and abilities of the Warbands during the Turns of both players in the coming Round. The total number of swords rolled on all the dice combined is the total amount of Power the player has to spend during the Round.

Players can spend as much Power as they like during a Turn and the dice can be used to track this. Any Power that is not spent by the end of the Round is discarded. See the table on page 20 for more detail about how and when Power can be used.

The End Phase

Once both players have finished activating all their models, including any Forced Fatigue (see pages 19 and 20), the Round concludes with the End Phase. During the End Phase, both players now perform the following steps in order:

1. Resolve all effects and abilities that state they take place in the End Phase.

2. Spend any remaining Power to clear Fatigue counters from models in their Warband. This is not mandatory however, a player is free to keep a model Fatigued if they wish.

3. In readiness for the next Round, clear away all activation counters from the table and any other counters (e.g. some spell effects) that are no longer required.

4. Any Power still unused at the end of this phase is discarded – it is not carried over to the next Round.

Activations

When a model is activated during a player's Turn, it may perform either one **long action** or up to two different **short actions**. Any model that is in the middle of its activation is called the acting, or active, model.

Note that unless specified otherwise by a Special Ability, rule, or by Force Fatiguing the model later (see page 20), a model may only perform each type of action once in a Turn.

A model that starts its activation Knocked-down, must *Stand Up* as its first action, even if Engaged.

The basic actions available to models in the game are listed below. Each action also indicates whether it is (short) or (long). An action must be completed fully before another can be taken.

Actions

Walk (short) – Only models that are not Engaged may take this action. Move the model up to its Speed in inches in any direction and leave it facing a desired direction. A *Walk* action must be performed even if the model is being simply turned on the spot to face a new direction. Models cannot move within 1" of enemy models unless they are Engaging one of them (see 'Engaged' opposite). See the full rules for Movement on page 22.

Shoot (short) – Only models with a ranged attack option (spell or weapon) and that are not Engaged may take this action. Target a single enemy model unless specified otherwise. The target must be in range, in the front arc of the firing model and the firing model must have LOS to the target. In addition, the target cannot be Engaged. See the Ranged attack rules on page 27.

Stand Up (short) – A model that is Knocked-down and is lying on the ground must *Stand Up* before it can take any other actions.

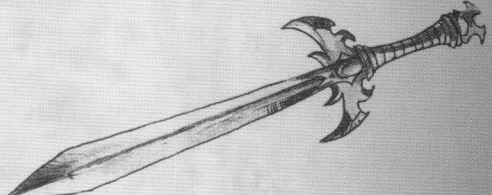

Melee (short) – The model makes a Melee attack against one model it is Engaged with in its front arc. Unless it intends to make a *Break Away* action, a standing model that is Engaged with one or more standing enemy models must perform a *Melee* action on one of those models. It may turn on the spot to put the target in its front arc if there is room for the base to fit. See the Melee attack rules on page 29.

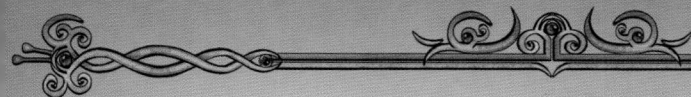

Cast (variable) – Only models that are not Engaged and with the SPELLCASTER Class can use the *Cast* action.

Note: *Cast* can be repeated as an action in a Turn.

The spell name will indicate if it takes a long or short action to cast. See Magic on page 40.

Run (long) – As a *Walk* action but the model may move up to twice its Speed in inches in any direction. If the model Engages an enemy model at the end of its move, the *Run* will qualify as a *Charge* action instead if both:

1. The moving model had Line of Sight (see page 25) to the Engaged enemy model before it moved.

2. It took the most direct route it could to the target, only deviating from a straight line to avoid Impassable Terrain or friendly models. In addition, the moving model cannot come within 1" of enemy models it is not going to Engage unless they themselves would be within 1" of the moving model's final position once Engaged.

If the move qualifies as a *Charge* action, the charging model gets an immediate free *Melee* action against the Engaged target.

Engaged

Models in base-to-base contact with a standing enemy model are **Engaged** by it. When a model moves to Engage another model, place the front of the moving model's base flush against the target's base on the side contact was made, as centrally as possible.

If a Group Charge (see page 20) is being performed, arrange the moving models as equally as possible if they are going to Engage the same target. Corner-to-corner base contact is not enough to Engage a model so is not a valid charge move for that target. See the Melee attack rules on page 29.

Only a qualifying Charge action to Engage an enemy model triggers a free Melee action.

A model that is Knocked-down cannot Engage an enemy model (but can be Engaged by one). See page 23 for more details.

A standing model that is Engaged by an enemy model can only make Melee or Break Away actions.

Engaging models behind obstacles

Sometimes a model will position itself so that it is touching an obstacle to put a barrier between it and any enemy models. It is still possible to Engage such a model and attack it. The attacking model must be able to move and reach the obstacle itself, make contact on the long edge of an obstacle and within 2" of the target model – there's no charging one end and then fighting a model way down the other end! If the moving model can achieve this, place it flush against the obstacle, directly opposite and facing the model it is going to attack.

Even if a model can move to within 2" of a target on the other side of an obstacle, there must still be room to move the model into position opposite to be Engaged. If other models are already Engaged and in the way, then the model cannot Engage the target. Project the edge of the target's base against the obstacle across it to determine how much space attacking models have to use.

Models that are Engaged across an obstacle are free to move away from one another without having to use a *Break Away* action.

Brace (long) – The model prepares and steels itself for an attack. The model may turn to face any direction but otherwise doesn't move or act in any other way. Its Armour is improved by one (e.g. 5+ becomes 4+) from any attack coming from its front arc until the model is next activated (place a Brace counter next to the model as a reminder).

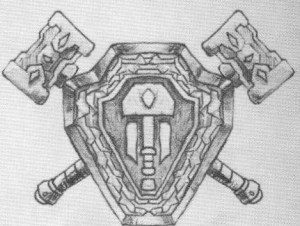

Break Away (long) – A model that is Engaged by one or more enemy models may attempt to break away instead of taking a *Melee* action. Make 1 unmodified Armour Roll (see page 30) for each enemy model the activating model is breaking away from. However, for each of these enemy models that is LARGE, instead make 2 unmodified Armour Rolls.

Models that are Knocked-down are ignored, as are any models that the model Breaking Away is wholly in the rear-arc of. The model will suffer a wound for each failed save. If the model is still alive and standing, it makes a *Run* action in any direction, following the normal movement rules. It may Engage another enemy model when doing so.

Fatigue

Sometimes, individuals in a Warband will push themselves to make an extra yard of ground, or fight that little bit harder. Such heroic efforts can come at the expense of exhaustion however, or finding yourself exposed.

During its activation, a model can be given an additional short action. This extra action must be taken after the model's "normal" actions for the Turn. It is known as a **Fatigue Action**, and the model is then marked as both Activated and **Fatigued** at the end of its activation (i.e. once all its actions and any attacks are resolved). A Fatigue Action cannot be a repeat of an action the model *already* made this Turn (this includes any free Melee action as a result of a Charge).

A Fatigue Action can also be given to a model that has already activated by spending Power as described below. This is known as "Forced Fatigue". See the table on page 20 for more details.

A Fatigue Action cannot be given to a group (see page 20), only to a single model. That is, you cannot combine Fatigue Actions with Group Actions. An activated member of a group may still receive a Forced Fatigue Action later by spending Power however.

If a model is marked as Fatigued at the start of its activation, it may only perform one short action. In addition, it cannot have a further Fatigue action played on it that Turn (although it may have Forced Fatigue played on it in a later Turn). Once the model's activation is complete, the model is marked as activated and the Fatigue counter it started the activation with is removed.

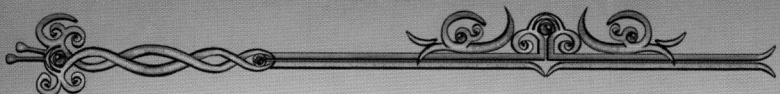

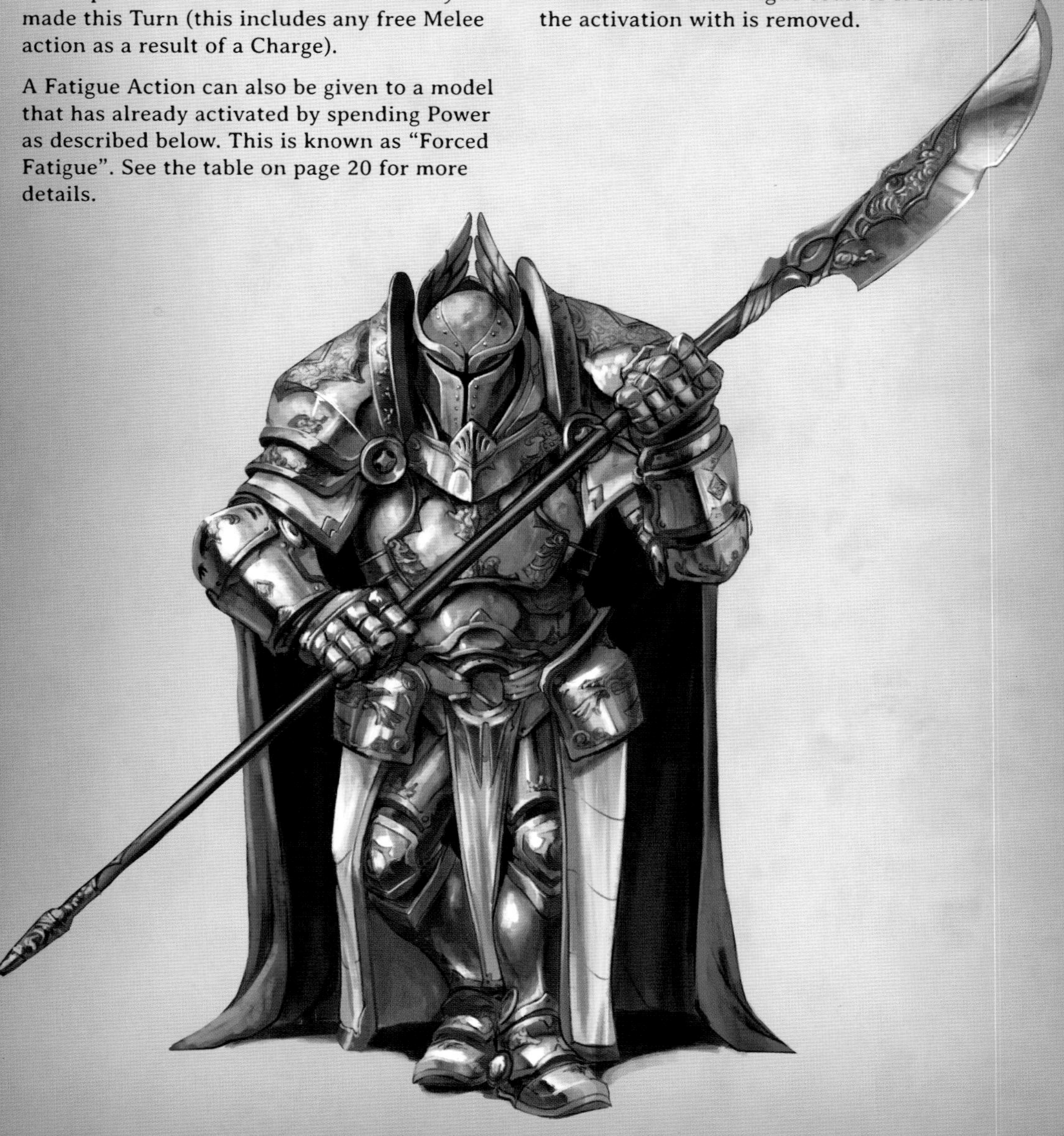

Standard Power Uses

Power Cost	Purchase	Description
1	+1 Model Activation	**What:** Activate a second model that has not yet been activated. Cannot be used to trigger a Group Action. **When:** After you have finished your first activation. You may only purchase one +1 Model Activation result per Turn. Unless specified otherwise by a model ability or Warband special rule, you may only activate a maximum of two models (or 1 model and 1 group) per Turn.
1	+1 Die	**What:** Add 1 bonus die to any of your Shoot, Cast, Armour Save or Melee rolls. **When:** Whenever you make a Shoot, Cast, Armour Save or Melee roll, including during your opponent's Turn (e.g. when Retaliating). The Power must be spent, and the bonus die added, before the roll is made. You may purchase a maximum of one extra die for a single dice roll.
1	Forced Fatigue Action	**What:** 1 Power may be spent to give any single model that has already activated this Round a "Fatigue" short action. **When:** The model chosen cannot already be Fatigued. Going back to a model to give it a Fatigue Action in this way is done instead of activating a model (or group) normally for a Turn (i.e. it replaces a normal activation). For the purposes of any rules or abilities, it is still considered an activation of the model. A Forced Fatigue action bought like this with Power CAN be a repeat of an action the model already performed earlier in the Round. A player may continue to buy Forced Fatigue Actions during a round even if all their models have activated normally until they declare they are finished for the Round.
1	Clear Fatigue	**What:** 1 Power may be spent to remove a Fatigue counter from a model in a player's Warband. Each Power spent clears one Fatigue counter. **When:** In the End Phase.
2	Group Defence (up to 3 models)	**What:** GROUP ACTION. The members of the group each make a Walk and then a Brace action. **When:** Spend the Power to nominate a group and activate them together. The group members must finish their movement within 3" of each other.
2	Group Shoot (up to 3 models)	**What:** GROUP ACTION. The group members may all either Walk then Shoot, or Shoot then Walk. If Shooting is a long action normally for any model in the group, that model may not Walk as part of the group action. All members of the group must have a ranged weapon or spell to use. **When:** Spend the Power to nominate a group and activate them together. The shooting models must all shoot the same target or different targets within 3" of each other. Shoot with all models in the group before Walking (or vice-versa). Shooting is resolved one at a time in any order you wish but all targets must be declared before dice are rolled.
2	Group Assault (up to 3 models)	**What:** GROUP ACTION. The group members all make a Run action and Engage an enemy model. **When:** Spend the Power to nominate a group and activate them together. Models in the group may already be Engaged (in which case they will not move, nor get any possible Charge bonuses). The group leader must have LOS to the initial target. Models moving after the first has made contact, must Engage either the same model another member of the group already has (or is already Engaged with), or a target within 3" of a model a group member has Engaged. Declare the targets and then move all the attacking models first, before resolving any free Melee actions for qualifying Charge actions in the order you wish. Models in the group that were already Engaged also make a single Melee action each. Any follow up moves for killing enemy models are performed after all attacks are resolved. Models in the group making follow up moves do not have to finish them within 3" of each other.
Various	Warband or Model Special Ability (n)	**What:** Use a Warband or model's Special Ability. The effect is different for each Warband or model and explained in the warband list or on the model's card. Special Abilities do not count towards any other restriction on the number of actions per Turn unless specifically mentioned otherwise (e.g. as a Group Action). The Power cost of the Special Ability will be given in brackets after its name. For example, a Special Ability with a (2) after it, requires 2 Power to use. **When:** The rules for abilities will indicate when you may spend Power to use the ability. Unless specified otherwise, a model with a Special Ability may only use it once per Round. They may use multiple abilities if they have them however. If a model dies, any Special Ability listed on its card can no longer be used. A Warband's Special Ability is always available to use however.

Using Power

Each Round, players have a limited resource of Power to spend and enhance the actions and abilities of their models. A player can spend as much of their Power as they wish to during a Turn.

To help keep track of Power, it's easiest to put the Power Dice to one side as you spend it. If you have a die result which shows a higher amount of Power than you want to spend, simply turn the die to the amount remaining (for example, from 2 swords down to 1).

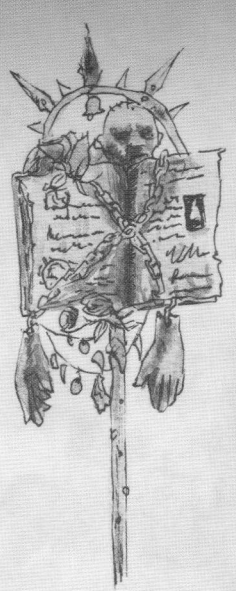

Spending Power

Players may spend their Power to "purchase" various options or activate special abilities. These might be specific to a model or Warband, or one of the standard uses from the table opposite.

Group Actions

Using Power, you can activate a group of models together. All models in the group must not have already been activated this Round. This is called a **Group Action** and all models are considered to be performing a long action for the Turn. Once the Group Action is complete, all models in the group are marked as activated.

To make a Group Action, nominate a model and then up to 2 more models within 3" of the first model. The selected models form the group. Some models have Special Abilities that are also Group Actions. The model with the Special Ability must be the nominated model of the group in order to use the ability.

Participating in a Group Action replaces a model's normal activation for the Turn. You cannot activate a single model, move it to join a group and then attempt a Group Action involving that model, for example.

The common Group Actions available to all models and Warbands are listed in the table opposite.

Model Special Abilities

Some models have Special Abilities. These will be described on the model's card or Warband entry, and cost Power to use as explained previously.

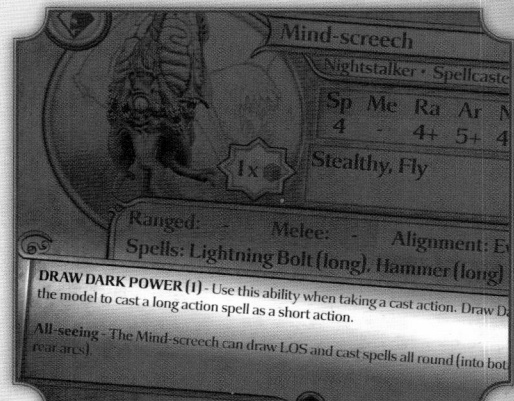

Warband Special Abilities

While the makeup of Warbands can and will be very different, every faction has a generic Special Ability that is always available to Warbands of that type.

Unless specified otherwise, Warband Special Abilities can only be used **once** per Round, at any time during one of that Warband's Turns.

Just like Model Special Abilities, these cost Power to use as explained earlier.

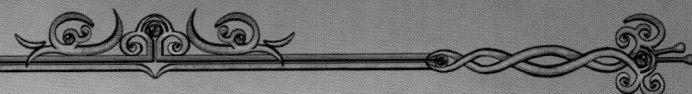

Sister Arvenia loosed another arrow. It struck one of the creatures in the chest. It screamed in what she could only assume was pain – a piercing shriek that tore into her mind like a serrated blade. Wincing through the noise, she nocked another arrow and loosed. This shaft stuck the creature's head, silencing its horrifying screams.

From her hidden vantage point at the forest's edge, she had a good position to see the rest of the ambush. Her sisters, supported by the men–at–arms of the local garrison, had tried to intercept an advancing group of the repulsive creatures. They didn't seem to have any kind of military organisation but they were vicious and utterly lethal. As she scanned for targets, she saw a swordsman hewn in two by a sickle-wielding spectral monstrosity. One of her sisters choked for air as her lungs were pierced by a dozen black claws.

At the centre of it all, the Abbess held firm. She wheeled and spun, cracking skulls and parrying claws with each movement, but always staying in the same place; refusing to yield a single step to these monsters. It was like seeing a single light standing against the darkness – a stirring sight for any daughter of Basilea.

Arvenia felt her blood run cold. Her spine tingled. Had she been flanked? There was no time to hesitate – she had seen first-hand how fast they were. She spun around, bow still drawn, ready to fire in a moment. The forest stretched out before her. Its boughs were dark and unnerving, its roots resembled tangled limbs. Nothing moved, there was no sound, no life of any kind. No threats. She stared into the gloom, trying to quiet her breathing. A cold sweat covered her skin as she tried to supress a shiver.

She never felt the blade sink into her back.

Movement

Moving your models around the battlefield is a vitally important part of the game if you want to ensure you have the right models in the right places and doing the job you need!

How far a model can move, in inches, will be stated in the action they are taking (see page 16).

Unless stated otherwise, models can move in any direction and turn as many times as they wish. Use a tape measure along the path the model is taking to determine how far it has moved.

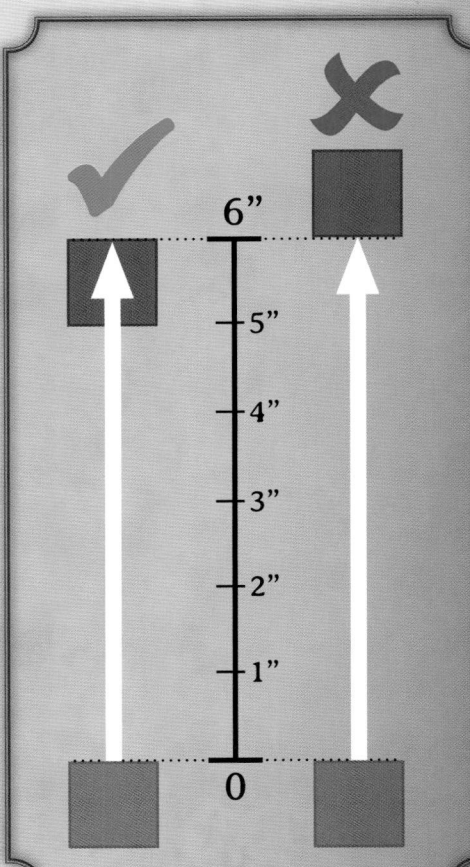

Make sure that at the end of the move the model is facing the direction you want it to as they cannot change facing after the action is over.

Unless a model is moving to Engage an enemy model, it may not move within 1" of any enemy models (See Run on page 17).

A model cannot move through any other models, including friendly ones.

Terrain on the table can affect the way models move. See the Terrain section on page 34 for more details.

Unless specified otherwise, models cannot leave the playing surface (treat the edges of the table as Impassable terrain).

Models ending their movement with their base touching an obstacle (e.g. a wall) must align one side of their base flush with it.

1) Move into contact

2) Align to obstacle

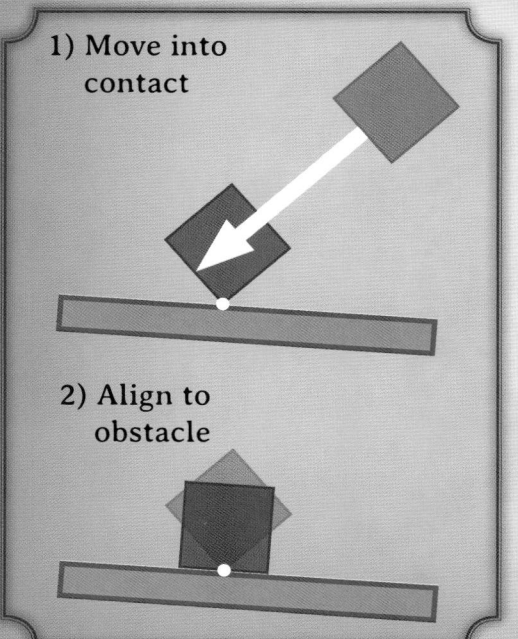

Knocked-down

Models that have been **Knocked-down**, are simply placed on their side where they stood. They lose any Brace counter they had and are considered to be half their normal Height (rounding down) for LOS purposes. They are still Engaged if they were before by any standing enemy models. Standing models in contact with a Knocked-down model are NOT Engaged by that model so can cast spells or make ranged attacks against it as well as make a Melee attack against it if they wish.

Any attacks against a model that is Knocked-down are considered to be from its rear arc.

A model that is Knocked-down and is lying on the ground must *Stand Up* before it can take any other actions.

Players may not wish to lay their painted models on the table (or there might not be enough space). In this case, place a marker next to the model to show its status.

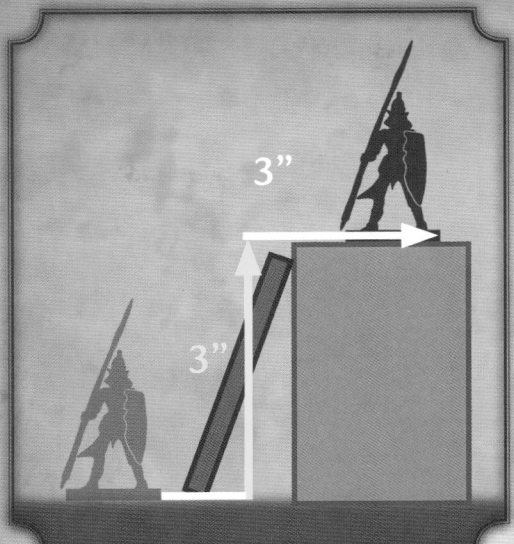

Strength *(n)*, where n is the difference in inches between the model's Height and the distance to the ground, rounding down.

Thus a Height 2 model pushed down a 4" high wall will take 2 hits from Falling, each with Crushing Strength (2). A Height 1 model moving down the same wall would take 3 hits from falling, each with Crushing Strength (3). A model that takes any wounds from Falling ends its action and is Knocked-down. See the special rules on page 38 for details on Crushing Strength.

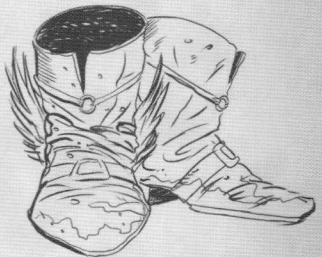

Vertical Movement

Moving up and down stairs has no penalty.

Models can **Climb** up or down ladders, counting the height of the ladder in inches as part of their movement.

Models can Climb up or down surfaces that the players have agreed require it, counting the height in inches of the surface being scaled as Difficult Terrain and part of their movement.

In both cases, they must reach the top (or bottom) by the end of their activation. Models cannot stop part-way up a wall, ladder or other surface during a Climb. A model that would end its movement at the top or bottom of a surface being climbed is considered to have successfully moved between levels and is placed at the appropriate end, with no further movement allowed as part of that action, but there must be sufficient room to place the model in position or the action cannot be performed.

Models of Class BEAST or with the special rule *Cavalry*, cannot Climb.

Dropping Down and Falling

On vertical surfaces, models can safely drop down their Height in inches without taking any injury (instead of a controlled Climb). This movement can be voluntary (e.g. dropping to a lower level) or involuntary (e.g. pushed off a cliff!). The vertical distance is counted as part of the model's movement. Models dropping further than their Height are **Falling** and take (n) hits with *Crushing*

Jumping

A model can **Jump** across gaps at the same level that are equal to or less than half its Sp value in inches but must make a test against its Sp value to do so and have sufficient movement to land and be placed on the opposite side. Roll a D8. If the result is equal or under the model's Sp value, the model successfully jumps the gap and may continue moving on the other side. Otherwise, the model Falls into the gap and may take damage as a result (see Falling above). The falling model is placed in the level it lands, directly below the point the jump was attempted from. Note that for this test, a roll of 8 is always a failure and 1 is always a success.

Arcs and Line of Sight

Arcs

Models in Vanguard are mounted on square bases, with the back edge of the base defining the **rear arc** of the model. To make it obvious which is the back edge, models should be glued to their base clearly facing one of the straight edges.

A model can potentially see anything in its **front arc** (subject to Line of Sight). Line of Sight (LOS) to anything wholly in the model's rear arc is considered to be **Blocked**.

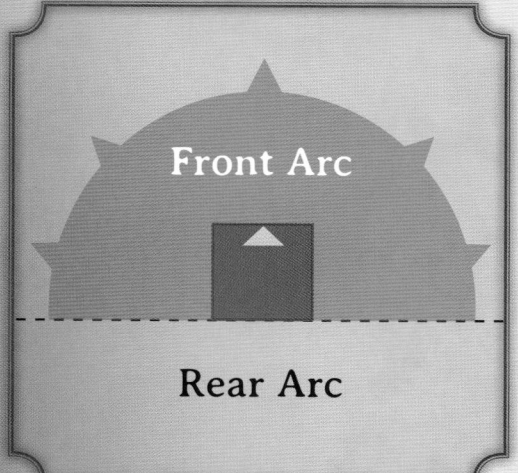

If a model is standing on (not in) terrain, then add the height of the terrain to the Height of the model when determining LOS.

Example: A model standing in an area of forest would not add the height of the forest to its own Height for LOS, but a model standing on the first floor of a building would add the height of that floor to its Height.

Line of Sight (LOS)

Even if something is in a model's front arc, other models and terrain may prevent the model from having LOS to it. A lumbering troll will most certainly block the view of a lowly goblin!

LOS is determined using a bird's eye view. If your model can draw an uninterrupted line from anywhere on its base to the whole of the enemy model's base then you have **Clear LOS**.

In most cases, it will be obvious if a model has LOS to something or not. In cases where it isn't however, all models and terrain have a Height which can be used to check for LOS.

As a general rule for terrain, each 1" of height is equivalent to 1 point of Height. For models, the Height is listed on their cards.

Models that are Knocked-down are considered to be half their normal Height (rounding down) for LOS purposes.

Blocked & Partially Blocked

Obviously on a battlefield there are many obstacles and pieces of cover that the enemy may utilise to protect themselves. The Height system is used to determine whether you still have LOS when you can't draw an uninterrupted line.

LOS from your model to an enemy model is considered Blocked if a line to all parts of the enemy model's base passes through:

- A model or terrain piece of the same height or more as your model, and the enemy model does not have a greater Height than the blocking item. (If the enemy model does have a greater height, LOS is only Partially Blocked) – see below.

- A blocking model or blocking terrain piece of the same height as the enemy model. However, this may be ignored if your model has a greater height than the blocking item and is within 3" of the blocking item.

- If LOS to an enemy model traces through more than 3" of Difficult Terrain that is equal or greater than its Height, LOS is Blocked.

LOS from your model to an enemy model is considered **Partially Blocked** if:

- Only part (not all) of the enemy model's base is in a position that would be considered Blocked.
- The enemy model is behind a blocking item but has a greater Height.
- The enemy model is within an area of Difficult Terrain that is at least Height 1 (e.g. shooting at a model within a wood).
- The enemy model is 3" or less within Difficult Terrain of equal or greater height.

An enemy model can be seen so long as LOS is either Clear or Partially Blocked. When LOS is Partially Blocked, the enemy model is often said to be "in cover".

Obstacles

A model in direct contact with, and tracing LOS over an obstacle that is of a lower Height than it, can ignore that obstacle for determining LOS. For example, an archer standing against a wall, firing over it, would not have their LOS blocked by the wall itself.

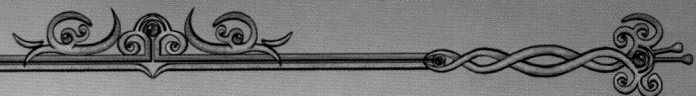

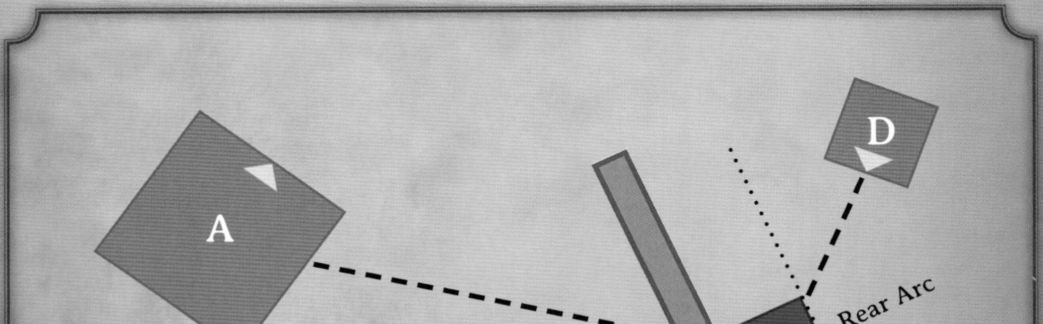

Models A and B can both see model X but in both cases, LOS is Partially Blocked by the Height 1 obstacle and/or the building. LOS from model C to model X is Blocked by the building. Model D has Clear LOS to model X.

Model X is in direct contact with and facing the obstacle, so can ignore it when tracing LOS across it. Therefore model X has Clear LOS to model A. LOS to model B is Partially Blocked by the building which also Blocks LOS to model C. LOS to model D is also Blocked because D is wholly within the rear arc of X.

Ranged Attacks

Whether your models are firing with bows, throwing knives, hurling arcane explosives or casting deadly spells, the following rules will explain how to resolve such attacks.

Ranged Attacks are made due to *Shoot* or *Cast* actions. Unless specified otherwise, a model may fire one weapon (or cast one spell) at a single enemy model with its action.

The target of a ranged attack must be in range and LOS of the firing model. Measure the distance from the base of the firing model to the base of the target model between the closest points. If the distance is equal to or less than the range value of the weapon, the target is in range. If LOS is blocked, the attack cannot be made.

Models can only make a *Shoot* action if they have a number of dice specified in their stats and are equipped with a Ranged weapon. If a model has a "-" listed for its Ra stat, it may not make a Ranged attack or be given any equipment of type Ranged.

A model may not fire at another model that is Engaged with a friendly model. A model that is Engaged itself may not make a Ranged attack.

If a model has more than one type of Ranged attack the player using the model must state which is being used before any dice are rolled.

To make the attack, the player rolls the number of dice shown in the model's Ranged section on its stat card (or equipment).

Modifiers and Bonuses

- If the firing model has a Clear LOS to the target model, the firing model receives one bonus die to add to its roll.

- If the firing model is standing on terrain that has elevated the model's Height to 3 or more Height levels higher than the target model, the firing model receives a +1 modifier to its roll.

For example, a Height 2 model standing on a Height 3 piece of terrain has a total Height of 5. It will gain a +1 modifier when shooting at models with a Height of 2 or less.

Each dice that equals or betters the Ra stat of the firing or casting model scores 1 hit on the target. The *Exploding 8s!* mechanism is used with each 8 result automatically scoring 1 hit.

Armour Roll

The owner of the target model then rolls 1 die for each hit scored. For each die that equals or betters the target's Armour value, 1 hit is ignored (saved).

The *Exploding 8s!* mechanism is used, with each 8 result automatically saving 1 hit.

Finally, the target model suffers one wound for each unsaved hit. If this takes the target to zero or less wounds, check the following conditions:

- If the model's Class is GRUNT it is removed from the table as a casualty and plays no further part in the game.

- Otherwise, a model on zero or fewer wounds must now make a Nerve test (see page 33). If the model has taken more wounds than it had remaining, the difference is used to modify the Nerve test. *For example, if a model with 1 wound suffers 2 wounds, the Nerve test has a -1 modifier:*

  - *Down But Not Out* - If the test is passed, the model survives with 1 wound remaining but is marked as fatigued (if not already). The model is additionally Knocked-down.

  - *Too Much Damage* - If the test is failed, the model is removed from the table as a casualty and plays no further part in the game.

Modifiers and Bonuses

- If the firing model's base is wholly in the rear arc of the target model, the attack gains *Piercing (1)* or increases the n value by 1 if the Ranged attack already has the *Piercing* special rule. Remember, if the target is Knocked-down, the attack is considered to be from the rear arc.

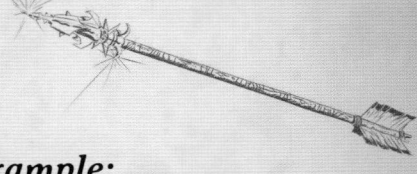

Example:

Player A's model takes a Shoot action at Player B's model. The model is determined to be within the range of the weapon and LOS to the target is Clear. The shooting model's Ranged section says to roll 2D8 and the model rolls an extra dice (3 in total) for the Clear LOS bonus. The model has an Ra stat of 5+.

Player A rolls the three D8s and scores 2, 6 and 8. The Exploding 8 means another die is rolled which scores a 4.

In total, the target is hit twice (the 6 and the 8).

Player B now rolls 2 dice for the Armour roll on the target. The target model's Armour is 6+. The dice score 4 and 7 so one hit is saved but the other one causes a wound on the target model.

Melee Attacks

A model that is in base to base contact with one or more enemy models is said to be Engaged.

A model that takes a *Melee* action makes a Melee attack against **one** enemy model it is engaged with and in its front arc. The owner of the attacking model chooses which enemy is being attacked if it is engaged with more than one enemy model.

Before any dice are rolled, the **attacking** player may turn their model on its centre to face any direction, so long as it remains in base contact with all the same enemy models and there is room to still fit the base in the new facing.

If a model has more than one type of Melee attack the player using the model must state which is being used before any dice are rolled.

To make the attack, the player rolls the number of dice shown in the model's Melee section on its card.

Modifiers and Bonuses

- If the attacking model Charged (*Charge* action) into the Melee this Turn, it gains 1 bonus die unless:
  - The target model is defending an obstacle
  - The charging model moved through Difficult Terrain or over an obstacle
- If the target model is Knocked-down, the attacking model gains a +1 modifier to its roll.
- Outnumbering: If one or more other friendly models, that are not Knocked-down or Fatigued, are also Engaging the target model, the attacking model adds 1 bonus die).

Each die that equals or betters the Me number of the attacking model causes 1 hit on the target. The *Exploding 8s!* mechanism is used with each 8 result automatically scoring 1 hit.

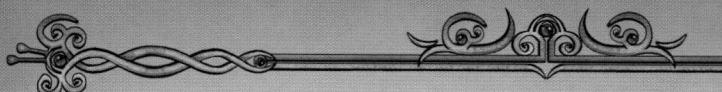

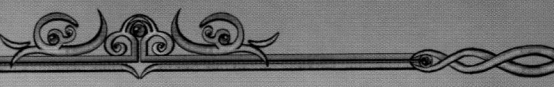
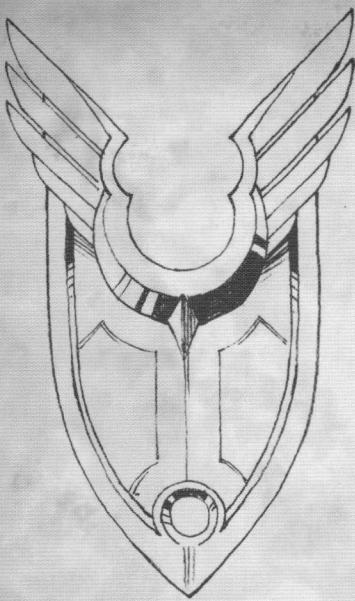

Armour Roll

The owner of the target model then rolls 1 die for each hit scored. For each die that equals or betters the target's Armour value, 1 hit is ignored (saved).

The *Exploding 8s!* mechanism is used, with each 8 result automatically saving 1 hit.

Finally, the target model loses one wound for each unsaved hit. If this takes the target to zero or less wounds, check the following conditions:

- If the model's Class is GRUNT **or it is already Knocked-down** it is removed from the table as a casualty and plays no further part in the game.

- Otherwise, a model on zero or fewer wounds must now make a Nerve test (see page 33). If the model has taken more wounds than it had remaining, the difference is used to modify the Nerve test. *For example, if a model with 1 wound suffers 2 wounds, the Nerve test has a -1 modifier:*

  - *Down But Not Out* - If the test is passed, the model survives with 1 wound remaining but is marked as fatigued (if not already). The model is additionally Knocked-down.

  - *Too Much Damage* - If the test is failed, the model is removed from the table as a casualty and plays no further part in the game.

Modifiers and Bonuses

- If the attacking model's base is wholly in the rear arc of the target when the move to Engage is declared (or is in the rear arc anyway while already Engaged), the resulting attack gains *Crushing Strength (1)* or increases the n value by 1 if the Melee attack already has *Crushing Strength*. Remember, if the target is Knocked-down, the attack will be considered to be from the rear arc.

- If the defending model is the other side of an obstacle and the attack is in its front arc, its Armour is improved by 1 for this Armour roll, as if it were Braced. A model already Braced will still receive this bonus.

Follow-up moves

If a model kills its enemy and there are no other enemy models in base-to-base contact with it, it may make a free **follow-up move** of 3" into its front arc, following the normal movement rules. However, when making a follow-up move, models are allowed to move within 1" of enemy models but they cannot contact and Engage them (models will often be fighting in tight conditions and will have to remain closer than normal to their enemies out of necessity). Models in a Group Assault action that kill their enemies and are no longer Engaged can each make a free follow-up move.

If a model kills its enemy and is still Engaged with other models, it may be turned to face any direction as long as it can still physically fit.

The goblins' intentions were clear. To overwhelm them in a rush and pin them down with sheer numbers, stopping them from being able to present a coordinated defence when the greenskins brought up their heavier troops. Indeed, behind the capering throng that hurtled towards him he could see the broad, hulking shape of a troll lumbering out of the tree line. A simple strategy, but one that could expose the main army to attack if ignored. In any other foe he would have found a grudging respect for their bravery, but the mindless green rabble could not be judged as other races. Brazak allowed himself a snort of derision and waited until the group of goblins was fully committed to their charge before issuing the order in a single, angular syllable.

Retaliate

A model that has been attacked in a *Melee* and has survived now has a chance to **Retaliate** and attack back. The intention to Retaliate is declared after the attack is resolved. If the model is being attacked by more than one enemy (for example as part of a Group Assault action), the intention to Retaliate is declared after each attack in turn but before the next one is resolved.

A model that is Knocked-down or that is already both Activated and Fatigued cannot Retaliate in a Melee. Therefore, a model may retaliate a maximum of two times during a Round.

To Retaliate, the model is turned so that the enemy model it is retaliating against is in its front arc. If there is no room to turn the model, it cannot Retaliate. It then makes a Melee Attack against its opponent as described above. Resolve the attack and then check the following conditions and use the first which applies:

1. If the retaliating model is not already marked as Fatigued, mark it as such with a Fatigued counter.

2. If the retaliating model has not already been marked as Activated this round mark it as such with an Activation counter.

If a retaliating model kills its opponent and is no longer engaged with any enemy models, it may make a follow-up move.

Models can't retaliate against a retaliation – once both models have struck blows, the *Melee* action is over.

Group Assaults

When resolving a Group Assault, the player whose models are attacking chooses the order to resolve each *Melee*. Each attack (and any Retaliation) is resolved fully before moving onto the next.

The three Ironclad warriors to his front moved as one, momentarily evoking the powerful, deliberate motion of the golem automata used by their dark kin. They braced their wide shields together in a perfectly executed Draz'nuth, the edges clattering against one another for a moment before becoming still and solid as a bastion wall.

The rabble of goblins did not break stride, however, and Brazak sneered beneath his beard as they rushed headlong towards the small shield wall that now protected the only entrance to the encampment. A desultory shower of arrows from some too-distant archers thudded into the earth around them or pattered harmlessly off their shields, their energy spent.

At the last moment the Ironclad squatted back on their haunches, then gave a massive shove to meet the goblins. With a shuddering crunch, small, green bodies burst in all directions as the goblin charge was stopped dead in its tracks. Brazak issued another curt instruction and the dwarfs took one, very deliberate, step forward into their disordered foes. Their hammers rose up, came crashing down, rose up again - this time caked with goblin blood - and fell once more.

Brazak did not know why the enemy were poking around the encampment and he did not much care. They would not get past his picket while he still breathed.

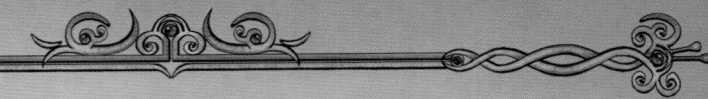

Nerve

A model's Nerve value is a representation of its morale, willpower and self-control. If things start to go wrong, or an individual is required to do something they aren't comfortable with, it might take a test of nerve to overcome it or the Warband will struggle to act as a coherent fighting force.

Nerve Tests

If the rules say a model must make a **Nerve test**, roll a single die and apply any modifiers given. If the result is equal or better than the model's Nerve stat, the test is passed. If it is under the model's Nerve stat, the test is failed.

Warband Morale

A Warband is **broken** if it has less than half the number of starting models remaining (by model count). Determine if a Warband is broken at the start of each Round.

Once a Warband is broken, each unengaged model in the Warband must make a **Fallback Check** the first time it activates in a Round. If performing a group action, use the Nerve value of the model nominated for the group to make the Fallback Check.

Fallback Checks

To make a Fallback Check, simply make a Nerve test.

If the test is passed, the Fallback Check is succesful and the model (or group) may be activated as normal.

If the test is failed, the Fallback Check is not successful and the model (or group) must make a special **Fallback!** action this Turn (see below).

If a group fails a Fallback Check, all group members must make a Fallback! action and must finish their moves within 3" of each other. Power must be spent on the Group Action **before** any Fallback Check is made.

A Fatigued model that fails its Fallback Check is marked as Fatigued again after the Fallback! action (i.e. it doesn't lose its Fatigue marker at the end of its activation).

Fallback!

A model making a *Fallback!* action, must move towards its own table edge (as defined by the scenario being played) along as direct a path as possible and as far as possible up to twice its Speed in inches (*Run*). If there is more than one Fallback edge defined for a warband, use the closest. A retreating model cannot engage enemy models and normal movement rules apply. Its Activation is then complete (mark it as activated).

Models that *Fallback!* may not have Fatigue Actions or Special Abilities played on them during their Activation. Power may be spent to give a model a Forced Fatigue Action later, however, without having to make another Fallback Check.

If a model that is falling back reaches the edge of the table (or started its *Fallback* there), it must make another Fallback Check immediately. If the test is passed, the model stops and is marked as activated. If it fails, it is removed from the board as a casualty.

If a model that is Knocked-down must *Fallback!* it will first *Stand Up* and then make a *Walk* action towards its own table edge.

TERRAIN

An empty battlefield might make moving models around simple but it's not very exciting! Adding scenery to your games makes for a dynamic and tactical experience that will help immerse you in the action. While you can use books to represent hills or a piece of card to mark the boundary of a small wood, having some great looking model terrain will really bring your games to life.

In Vanguard, the different types of scenery and terrain used are classified into the following categories:

Open Ground

Areas of flat open grass, road, or any other clear swathe of land is considered to be Open Ground. Open Ground doesn't impede a model's movement in any way.

Obstacles will often provide cover for targets behind them as they can cause LOS (see page 25) to be Partially Blocked.

Models standing at windows treat them as obstacles for all purposes.

Obstacles

Obstacles are linear barriers that may lie in a model's path as it moves. Examples are walls, hedges and fences. Obstacles up to the height of the model cost 2" of movement to cross over, regardless of how fast the model is moving. Anything taller than the model will need to be climbed up and over.

Difficult Terrain

Areas of broken ground, wooded areas, ruins, steep scree slopes and marshy ground are all examples of Difficult Terrain. Models count every inch moved in Difficult Terrain as 2". Thus, a model moving 3" through Difficult Terrain counts as having moved 6".

Areas of Difficult Terrain should be clearly defined with an obvious boundary. Unless the players agree, or a scenario specifies an exact configuration of the elements within the area, they are simply representations and can be moved to make model placement easier if required (e.g. you may need to move a tree to one side to make room for a model that has moved).

Impassable Terrain

Some terrain simply blocks movement. Solid buildings, lava pools, large rock pillars are all good examples. Models cannot move into or on top of Impassable Terrain and must move around it.

Terrain Heights

Terrain will have a Height, just like models do and so will interact with the LOS rules in the same way.

Players should agree what Height each piece of terrain they are using will be before they play a game. Because everyone has different terrain collections, the following table should be considered a guideline to defining terrain in your games, rather than hard and fast rules.

Feature	Height
Floor	0
Walls, Hedges, Fences, areas of low-lying ruins and boulders, heavy scrubland etc.	1
Gentle hill	2
Wood	5+
Single storey building/ruin	4
2-storey building/ruin	6

SPECIAL RULES

Some models, spells, effects and attacks make use of a collection of abilities known as Special Rules. Each of these Special Rules is an exception to the normal rules. The most common are listed below. Rules unique to a model will be printed on its reference card.

6th Sense

A standing model with this rule attacked by Melee in their rear arc may turn to face the attacker, which occurs before any Melee attack is resolved. The attacking model loses any bonus for attacking from the rear. A model Engaged with any other enemy model may not use this rule.

Area Effect (range / dice / rules)

Attacks that have the *Area Effect* rule may also hit models near to the original target and at the same Terrain Height the target is currently on or in. The *Area Effect* rule will detail the size of the affected area, how many attack dice are rolled and any Special Rules that may apply (note that the Special Rules from the initial attack don't automatically apply). Once any damage and effects on the original target are resolved, the extended area effect attacks are then resolved in any order the player using the attack wishes.

For example, if an attack has *Area Effect* (2" / 2D8 / Piercing (1))*, all models (not just enemy ones!) within 2" of the original target would be attacked with 2D8 and any hits resolved with *Piercing (1)*. Roll for each model separately. *Area Effect* attacks on a model other than the original target are always assumed to be from the direction of the original target.

If the original target is killed, leave it in place until all *Area Effect* hits have been measured and resolved, then remove it.

Unless specified otherwise, models can only avoid being hit by an *Area Effect* attack if LOS to them from the original target would be blocked by impassable Terrain. Assume the original target has full LOS into both front and rear arcs for working this out. No bonus die for Clear LOS is granted however.

Breath

Using the width of the firing model's base, extend a rectangle out to the range of the attack. Unless LOS is blocked to them, make separate attack rolls against all models whose bases are partially or wholly inside the designated area. No bonus die is granted for Clear LOS however. A *Breath* attack may be targeted at the same Terrain Height the firing model is in or on, or 1 Height either way (e.g. firing up or down a level). The attack will affect all the models in the area of the *Breath*, on or in the target Height. *For example, a Height 2 model standing in a Height 2 ruin (total Height 4) could choose to target its Breath attack at any Height from 1 to 5.*

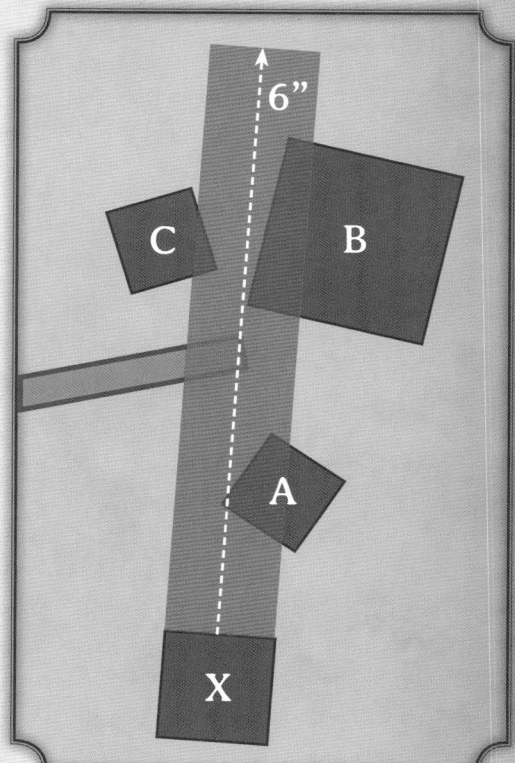

Model X uses an attack with a 6" Breath. Models A and B are both attacked. While model C is within the template, LOS is Blocked by a Height 4 wall and so model C is not attacked.

Bloodlust

Models with this rule add 1 bonus die to their Melee attack if the model they are attacking has already suffered one or more wounds.

Cavalry

Models with this rule receive a +1 modifier when making Melee attacks against models of a lower Height (including any Terrain). They cannot Climb however, and will automatically Fall if they attempt to Climb down a surface.

Crushing Strength (n)

Melee attacks from models or weapons with this rule apply a -(n) modifier to the target's Armour Roll when attempting to save against hits. For example, an attack made with *Crushing Strength (1)* would change a roll of 5 to 4.

Defender

Brace is a short action for models with this special rule.

Dodge

When targeted by a Ranged attack, the player owning the target model can force the attacking player to re-roll one die that caused a hit. This can be used to re-roll an Exploding 8 to try and prevent it Exploding!

Fly

Models with this special rule can move over other models and terrain that would normally block their way. They can also move up or down a number of levels of height up to their Sp value with no penalty (or chance of injury). However, they still cannot end their move on impassable terrain or other models.

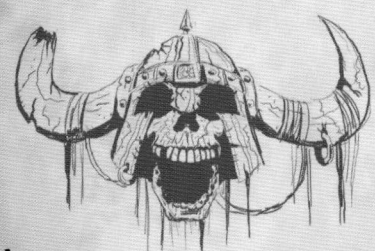

Headstrong

If a model with this special rule is Fatigued, when it is activated, roll a die. On a 6+, the Fatigue counter is removed and the model may act as normal.

Inspiring

A model with this rule, and all friendly models within 6" of it, may re-roll failed Nerve tests.

Marksman

A model with this rule can re-roll any 1s when making Ranged attacks.

Mob Assault

When involved in a Group Assault action, all models with this rule taking part gain *Crushing Strength (n)*, where n is the number of models in the group sharing this rule and attacking the same target. Thus, two models attacking would each have *Crushing Strength (2)*. Calculate this before each attack, allowing Retaliate to reduce the effects by killing members of the assaulting mob.

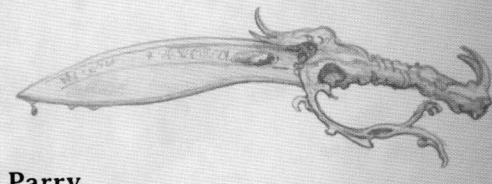

Parry

When targeted in Melee, which includes Retaliate, the player owning the target model can force the attacking player to re-roll one die that scored a hit. This can be used to re-roll an Exploding 8 to try and prevent it Exploding!

Pathfinder

Models with this rule treat any Difficult Terrain they move through as Open Ground (including in a *Charge* action).

Piercing (n)

Ranged attacks from models or weapons with this rule apply a -(n) modifier to the target's Armour Roll when attempting to save against hits. For example, an attack made with *Piercing (2)* would change a roll of 7 to 5.

Pound

If an attack with this rule scores 3 or more hits and the target is not killed, it is Knocked-down. Apply this rule after any possible *Down But Not Out* result.

Regenerate (n+)

When a model with this rule activates for the first time in a Round, roll a die. If the result is equal to or better than the n value, the model recovers one wound previously suffered in the game

Reload

Shoot is a long action for any Ranged weapons with the *Reload* rule. However, the model may pivot on the spot before making an attack.

Scout

After all standard model deployments have been made, but before the game starts, models with the *Scout* skill may set up outside their deployment area but not within 12" of the enemy deployment area or 12" of an enemy model. If both players have models with *Scout*, the player that finished deploying their other models first chooses the first *Scout* model to be deployed – the players then alternate placing their Scouts. Models with *Scout* may always be placed in their own deployment area if desired.

Smash

A model with this rule gains the *Pound* special rule in the subsequent Melee attack when it performs a *Charge* action.

Sneaky

When attacking the rear arc of a model in Melee, rolls of 7 or 8 are Exploding! and therefore score a hit and can be rerolled.

Steady

If a model with this rule is Knocked-down, roll a die. On a 5+, the model remains standing.

Stealthy

When making Ranged attacks at a model with this rule, attacking models suffer a -1 modifier when rolling for hits (including casting spells).

Stubborn

A model with this rule may re-roll failed Nerve tests.

Swarm

When contributing to an outnumbering bonus for another models Melee attack, models with this rule grant 2 bonus dice.

Unbreakable

A model with with this rule automatically passes any Fallback Check it is required to make for any reason.

Very Inspiring

A model with this rule, and all friendly models within 9" of it, may re-roll failed Nerve tests.

Vicious

A model with this rule can re-roll any 1s when making Melee attacks.

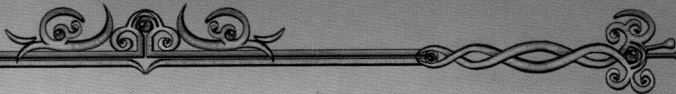

MAGIC

In the fantasy setting of Vanguard, certain talented (or warped!) individuals can harness and utilise arcane and mysterious magical powers.

Casting spells

In the game, models with the ability to cast magical spells have the SPELLCASTER Class.

All spells are Ranged Attacks using a *Cast* action. Unless specified otherwise, normal LOS, ranged targeting rules and damage resolution apply. A spell will specify after its name if it takes a short or long *Cast* action to use. Unless also specified otherwise, spells roll to attack using the Ra of the casting model.

A model may use the *Cast* action more than once in its activation. However, a model may not cast the same spell more than once in a Turn.

The most common spells are listed on the following pages. Spells unique to a model will be printed on their stat card. Typically, models will only be able to use a small number of spells, as specified on their card.

Each spell description will state the Range of the spell (if applicable), how many dice to roll and then any special or unique rules that apply.

Boosted Spells

Some spells can be Boosted by Special Abilities, by Power directly (in addition to the normal action cost), or by taking a longer action. This will be detailed in the spell description, or the Special Ability. Where a model has a Special Ability that can boost a spell (e.g. extending the range), and the spell can be boosted itself, it is possible to do both, so long as the appropriate action is taken, and Power spent.

If a model has a Special Ability that boosts a spell's range, it will only affect spells that explicitly list a Range (e.g. [Range 12"]).

If a model is listed as having a spell, it automatically has access to the boosted version too, where the spell has one.

Ongoing Spell Effects

Some spells have delayed or lasting effects. Spell Effect counters are provided to help track models that have these spells cast on them. Unless specified otherwise in the spell description, Spell Effect counters should be removed from the board in the End Phase, ending any effect they may have caused.

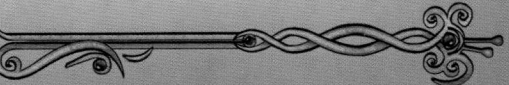

Vanguard Basic Spellbook

The following list details the Vanguard Basic Spellbook. Additional spells are available if you are playing a campaign, as spellcasters gain experience and learn new incantations and tricks. There are also options for gaining new spells in one-off games. See page 122 and 144 for more details.

Fireball (short): Range 9", 2D8

Boosted version: Cast as a long action instead to add the *Breath* Special Rule to the spell for this casting.

Hammer (long): Range 12", 2D8

If any hits are scored, no wounds are caused. Instead, the target is Knocked-down.

Heal (short): Range 6"

Target a single friendly model in range (but not the caster), even if it is Engaged, and roll 3D8. For each 6+ rolled, the target recovers 1 wound previously suffered.

Boosted version: Cast as a long action instead. As above, but for each 5+ rolled on this casting, the target recovers 1 wound previously suffered.

Lightning Bolt (long): Range 12", 3D8, Piercing (1), Marksman

Boosted version: Cost 2 Power. As above, but the attack gains the *Area Effect* (2" / 2D8) special rule for this casting.

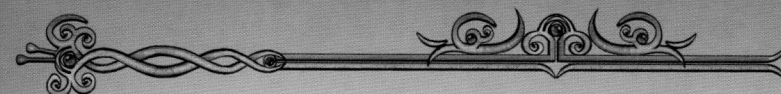

41

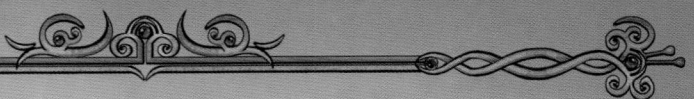

Mind Storm (long): Range 6", 2D8, Piercing (1)

LOS is not required to the target to cast this spell.

Shield (short)

Cast on self. No dice roll required. Caster gains the *Stealthy* Special Rule and decreases its Armour value by 1 until the end of the round (e.g. Ar 5+ becomes 4+). Place a Spell Effect marker on the target as a reminder.

Shockwave (long)

All models (including friendly ones) of up to Height 2 within 3" of the caster are moved 3" directly away from the caster. Movement will only be blocked by Impassable Terrain or other models not affected by the Shockwave. Move the models furthest away from the caster first. Models cannot become Engaged when moved by Shockwave – halt them 1" away if they would be. Models already Engaged will still end up Engaged with each other if both are moved.

> Boosted version: Cost 1 Power. As above, but models up to Height 3 are affected for this casting.

Stun (short): Range 12", 2D8

If any hits are scored, no wounds are caused. Instead, the target is marked as Fatigued.

Windblast (long): Range 9", 3D8

No wounds are caused. Instead, for each hit scored, the target model is pushed back 3" directly away from the caster stopping only for Impassable terrain or other models. If a model is pushed into an enemy model, it stops and is Engaged.

Zap (short): Range 12", 3D8

> Boosted version: Cast as a long action instead. As above, but the spell has the *Piercing (1)* special rule for this attack.

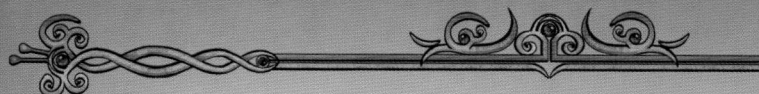

The filthy slavers had outfoxed them. Damian knew his scouting party had tracked them without detection. All his experience told him he was right.

The screams and carnage in front of him told him otherwise.

As the last of the terrified townsfolk fled across the square towards Damian's crew, who were sheltering behind a blockade they had hastily erected at the north gate to shield the escape, a dwarf woman clutching a child tripped and staggered into an over-turned market stall. Crashing to the ground to howls of delight from her pursuers, she clung hard to the child, even as the whips lashed round her ankles and dragged her bloodily towards the snarling warriors that were now running into the cobbled market.

"Not on my watch." The upturned cart threatened to topple over as Arthur leapt the obstacle and sprinted towards the stricken dwarf. His twin Amelia stood, nocked an arrow, and let fly all in one fluid motion. The missile struck the slaver with unnerving accuracy, burying itself through the eye slit of a tarnished helmet and eliciting an audible snap from the dark elf's neck. The distraction gave Arthur the chance he needed to dive for cover and roll towards the outstretched arms of the panicking mother who had realised his goal. Tearing the child from her arms, he spun away and almost dropped the boy as arrows skipped off the ground by his feet. Racing back to the makeshift defences, he vaulted the cart and took a glancing blow to his shoulder as another arrow blurred through the air and into the open window of a nearby shop. The screams of the babe were echoed on the other side of the square as its mother was dragged to a life of hellish torment.

"Brace!" Two shadows detached themselves from the corner of the square and solidified into dark elves, faces hidden by black cloth. The hatred that fuelled their lethal intent was almost palpable as first one and then the other pounced against the barricade's defenders with a feline grace. The kin were known to coat the edges of their weapons in poisons and bodily waste so that even the mildest of cuts might result in their victims succumbing to the ravages of a hideous toxin or infection. Blades the colour of night whirled and slashed at the faces of Damian's beleaguered warband and they desperately parried and held their ground against the onslaught.

With a roar, Tuvook, the orge mercenary currently contracted to the warband, reached across and caught the forearm of one elf and hauled it towards him. With a grimace, he slammed his massive fist into the face of the elf

with a sickening crunch and hauled the limp body over the cart and onto the floor. Damian had slit the creature's throat almost before it hit the deck.

More elves had poured into the square and now at least half a dozen were at the cart, a baying, frenzied mob. To Damian's left, Amelia winced as a spear breached the lines and tore a crimson slash across her cheek. Next to her, Vargus hoisted himself onto the cart and loosed an arrow from his hunting bow at almost point blank range into the chest of a tattooed blade-dancer, only for him to be immediately hacked almost in two by a mighty blow from an unseen halberd.

An ungodly cacophony reverberated around the square, cutting through the din of battle. In the far distance, a stooped, fragile being stepped over the body of a market trader. A black, multi-headed monstrosity paced at the crone's feet and stopped to feast on the corpse, entrails dripping from its wicked teeth. The dark elf sorceress raised her eyes to the skies and screamed aloud once more, arms to the heavens. An unnatural silence washed through the square accompanied by the acrid stench of ozone.

"Run!"

Too late. The Nightstalker reaper that had been summoned smashed through the wall behind the defenders. Its blind head scanned the warriors in front of it for a brief second before it lunged forwards, lashing out in all directions with teeth, claw and blade. Arthur screamed and dropped the child he was holding as the reaper's serrated limbs punched through his body and pinned him to the wall. In almost the same motion it decapitated Rydiger, the dwarf ranger, a veteran of seventy-five years of combat. The reaper screamed as its body jerked wildly, trying to extricate itself from the wall its blade-like limbs were now buried in.

Instinct kicked in, and grabbing the child on the floor, praying it was not hurt, Damian screamed at the remains of his warband and ran. They fled, leaving their wounded to an unthinkable fate as the tide of elves rolled over the barricade and set about them. They had been a good crew. They still would be. Damian passed the child to Amelia and locked her gaze. They'd known each other for years. She knew what he intended to do and merely nodded. Shouting her instructions, she fled.

Damian turned back to face the slavers. The Twilight Kin. Knife in one hand and sword in the other, he steadied his breathing, wiped sweat from his brow, and prepared to buy his warband as much time as he possibly could.

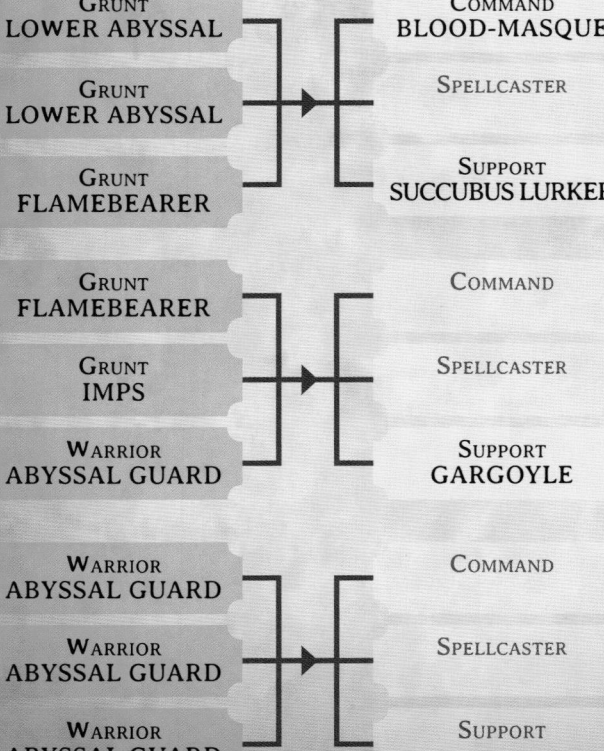

GRUNT LOWER ABYSSAL	COMMAND BLOOD-MASQUE
GRUNT LOWER ABYSSAL	SPELLCASTER
GRUNT FLAMEBEARER	SUPPORT SUCCUBUS LURKER
GRUNT FLAMEBEARER	COMMAND
GRUNT IMPS	SPELLCASTER
WARRIOR ABYSSAL GUARD	SUPPORT GARGOYLE
WARRIOR ABYSSAL GUARD	COMMAND
WARRIOR ABYSSAL GUARD	SPELLCASTER
WARRIOR ABYSSAL GUARD	SUPPORT

Example Abyssal Warband:

Narahkt's Hell-Raisers

Hellequin Blood-Masque	42 pts
+ Blade of Slashing	4 pts
+ Healing Herbs	3 pts
Lower Abyssal	8 pts
Lower Abyssal	8 pts
Flamebearer	9 pts
Flamebearer	9 pts
Imps	13 pts
Abyssal Guard	14 pts
Abyssal Guard	14 pts
Abyssal Guard	14 pts
Abyssal Guard	14 pts
+ Large Shield	3 pts
Succubus Lurker	24 pts
+ Bandages	2 pts
+ Lucky Charm	1 pts
Gargoyle	18 pts
TOTAL	**200 pts**

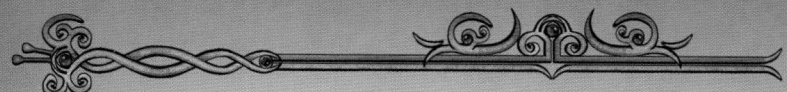

CREATING A WARBAND

You can play Vanguard with just a few models per player, without worrying about the two sides being equally matched. This is great for learning the game, but after you've become familiar with the rules and have amassed a larger collection of models, you will want to play games where the forces facing one another across the battlefield are balanced, so that both players have an equal chance of winning the game (at least to start with!).

In order to achieve this, you and your opponent must pick a Warband before the game by spending a number of 'points'. Both players have 200 points to spend on their Warband for a game unless the scenario being played specifies otherwise. However, once players are familiar with the game they may wish to experiment and play larger or smaller games with different points values.

Each player picks models from one of the faction lists provided in this book, or from their deck of Vanguard Warband cards for the faction. Each model costs a certain amount of points, as shown in its entry or card. More powerful or specialist models will cost more points. You may also buy additional equipment for your Warband (see page 120).

As you pick models and equipment items and include them in your Warband, keep adding their cost until you have reached the total you agreed. You can of course spend less than the agreed total, but you cannot spend even a single point more. However, a Warband is still considered to be the size of the maximum total the players agreed on (e.g. a Warband which comes to 197 points would still be considered a 200 point Warband).

Warband Selection

In order to restrict the possible (nasty!) combinations that can be fielded and to make sure Warbands have a semblance of 'realism' about them, the following limitations are placed on the model Classes and numbers that can make up your Warband:

- You must take a minimum of 5 WARRIORS and/or GRUNT models and 1 COMMAND model.

- You may take up to 1 COMMAND, 1 SUPPORT and 1 SPELLCASTER model for every 3 WARRIOR and/or GRUNT models you select.

- You may take up to 1 LARGE model for every full 150 points in the Warband. However, the first COMMAND model that is also LARGE in the Warband does not count against this limit.

- You may take up to 1 of each different type of model (as defined by their cards) for every full 40 points in the Warband. Thus in a 200 point game, you can select a maximum of 5 of each type of model (e.g. 5 Goblin Rabble, 5 Mawbeasts etc.)

- If a model has more than one Class (e.g. SUPPORT and SPELLCASTER), it counts as 1 of each for the purposes of selection within a Warband.

Models with a * after their name are unique Named Characters. Only one model with a * in its name may be taken in a Warband.

Smaller Games

When you are learning to play, or if you just want a quick fun game with a handful of models, you can modify the selection rules above as follows, recommended for games of 100 points per side or less:

- You must take a minimum of 2 WARRIORS.

- You do not have to take any COMMAND models but may always take one if you wish.

- You may take a maximum of 1 LARGE model.

Because smaller games do not insist on COMMAND models, remember that this means a warband might not be able to re-roll its Power Dice at the start of each Round!

GAME SCENARIOS

Games of Vanguard are played on a space 3' x 3' square. The scenarios presented on the following pages assume this size of playing area when describing their set up. Experienced players may choose to play on larger or smaller areas once they are more familiar with the rules and want to try something different.

Although some scenarios may differ, the standard steps for preparing for a game of Vanguard are as follows:

1) Prepare your Warband

First of all, you and your opponent must select your Warbands, up to a limit of 200 points, as described on page 45.

2) Determine Scenario

Each scenario will have a different objective for the players to complete in order to win the game (and thwart their opponent!). You may either mutually agree which scenario you will play, or you can roll randomly as described below.

Roll a D8 and note the result. Now roll a second D8. If this scores a 5 or higher, add 8 to the first D8 result, otherwise the first result is unadjusted.

Now consult your result of 1 to 16 on the following table to see which scenario will be played.

Result	Scenario
1-2	Supply Grab
3-4	Light the Beacon
5-6	Free the Princess
7-8	Recover the Plans
9	Kill the Bard!
10	The Dragon's Egg
11	The Power Stones
12	Capture the Giant!
13	Destroy the Baggage Train
14	Burn the Stores
15	Secure the Portal
16	Kill the Commander

3) Place Terrain

Before the game, it's a good idea for you and your opponent to have some terrain ready to put on the battlefield. Take it in turns to place the terrain, or ask a third-party to place it for you. Arrange it in a sensible manner, aiming to recreate a plausible landscape of the fantastic and dangerous world your Warbands are operating in and at least 25% coverage on the table. Some scenarios may dictate some terrain elements for you.

During this stage it is vital that you agree with your opponent what each piece of terrain is going to be during the game – Difficult, Blocking etc. Also agree terrain heights.

4) Set up

After rolling for the scenario and placing terrain, any required objective counters or scenario-specific items should be placed as instructed. Both players now roll a die. Re-roll any ties. The player scoring highest now chooses which side of the table will be theirs and places (deploys) one of their models onto the battlefield no more than 4" on from their chosen table edge (some scenarios may have different deployment areas). Their opponent does the same on their opposite side of the table. The players keep alternating in doing this until they have placed all of their models onto the table. The Fallback table edges for each player will be highlighted on the scenario map.

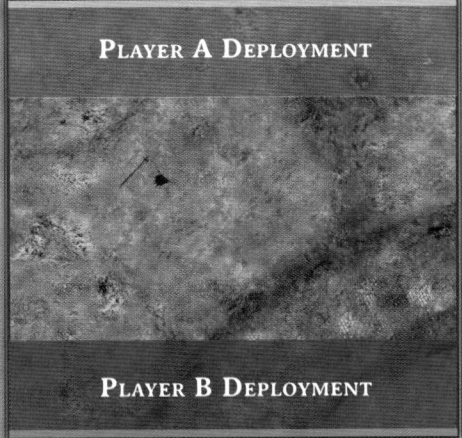

PLAYER A FALLBACK EDGE

PLAYER A DEPLOYMENT

PLAYER B DEPLOYMENT

PLAYER B FALLBACK EDGE

5) Who goes first?

Both players now roll a die. The player that finished deploying their models first, adds 1 to their result. Re-roll any ties. The player that scores the highest chooses who takes the first Turn in the first Round.

6) Duration

Play the game for 5 Rounds.

At the end of Round 5, the player that finished activating their models first rolls a D8. On a roll of 1-5, the game ends. On a roll of 6 or more, one more Round is played and then the game ends.

If one side wipes out the other before the last Round ends, the rest of the current Round is played to completion and then the game ends.

7) The Winner

The scenario being played will tell you what the victory conditions are to determine the winner.

Game on!

Kings of War

Vanguard is all about the events that take place before, between and after major battles. They are part of a bigger story and by combining games of Vanguard with Mantic's Kings of War, this larger narrative can be explored.

In each of the scenarios that follow, there is a Kings of War story "hook" presented which will tie the result of your Vanguard games into your next linked Kings of War battle against the same opponent and enemy army. Some results might have effects for both sides! See the section of combining Kings of War and Vanguard games for more detail (page 155).

1. SUPPLY GRAB

A raid on a resupply to one of the armies has resulted in the few remaining supplies scattered in the wild. One side desperately needs to retrieve what remains to bring it back to their ailing forces and the other side is determined to stop them, thus further weakening the enemy army.

Set up

Place 3 objective counters on the table to represent the scattered remaining supplies – these can simply be coins, or models representing weapons, food, treasure or similar. Counters should not be larger than 40mm across. Place one in the centre of the table between the players, and the others 12" away in either direction from the central one and 4" towards the players as shown below.

Now deploy the forces using the standard set-up as described on page 48.

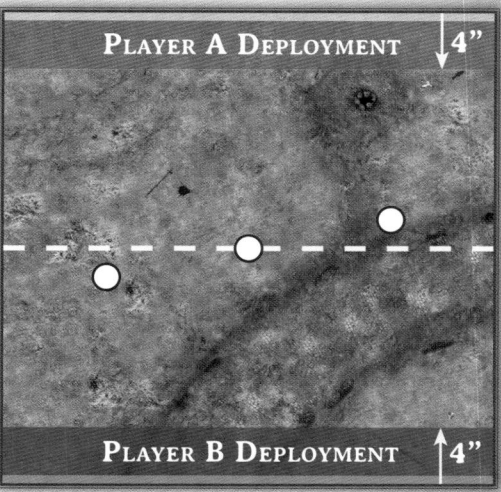

PLAYER A DEPLOYMENT ↓4"

PLAYER B DEPLOYMENT ↑4"

The Winner

Both players are aiming to capture the objectives. The centre one is worth 3 Victory Points (VPs). The outer ones are worth 2 VPs each.

Calculate the VP scores for each side at the end of the game. The player with the most VPs wins.

Kings of War Hook

Both players will earn supplies in relation to the number and value of objectives they capture.

For the next KoW battle, each player gains an additional number of points to spend on their army equal to 1% of the army multiplied by the number of VPs they scored.

For Example: Player A captures objectives totalling 4VP. With a 2000 point KoW game to play, 1% of 2000 is 20 points. Multiplied by 4 VPs gives 20x4 = 80 extra points to spend. Thus Player A can select an army up to 2080 points.

Scenario Rules

To capture an objective, a model must be in base contact with it, standing, not Engaged and with no enemy models in base contact with the same objective. In any other condition, an objective cannot be claimed.

Objective counters are static, don't block movement or LOS and cannot be picked up or moved.

Alternate game

Try playing with 5 objective counters instead of 3. Place 1 in the middle worth 3 VPs and then the players take it in turns to place the others outside deployment areas and not within 6" of another counter. These are worth 1VP each.

2. LIGHT THE BEACON

High upon the hills of Mantica stand signal beacons used to call allies in times of need. Just such a beacon has been captured by an invading force's smaller warband, guarding it to prevent reinforcements being summoned for the main battle in the days ahead. Can the attackers break the enemy lines and light the signal to call forth help?

Set up

Roll-off to decide who will be the Attacker and who will be the Defender. The Attacker selects a warband to 200 points, the Defender to 175 points.

Place the beacon objective marker centrally on the table 6" in from the Defending player's table edge. Place it on a small Height 2 hill. The beacon starts the game unlit. The area between the two deployment zones should be filled with a variety of ruins, walls and some light wooded areas – about 30% coverage.

The Attacker completes all their deployment first, then the Defender places all of their models. Up to two WARRIOR or GRUNT models from the Defender's force may be placed in contact with the beacon. All other defending models must be deployed more than 12" from it and within the Defender's deployment area.

The *Scout* special rule cannot be used in this scenario.

The Defender takes the first Turn in the first Round.

The Winner

The Attacking player wins if the beacon is alight at the end of the last Round.

The Defending player wins if the beacon is not lit or has been put out (doused) by the end of the last Round.

Scenario Rules

To interact with the beacon, a model must be standing in base contact with it, not Engaged and with no enemy models in base contact with the beacon. A model may take a long action to light or douse the beacon. The beacon objective marker is a static piece of Height 4 Impassable Terrain that blocks LOS.

Use a marker or better, a removable flame model, to show the current status of the beacon – lit or unlit.

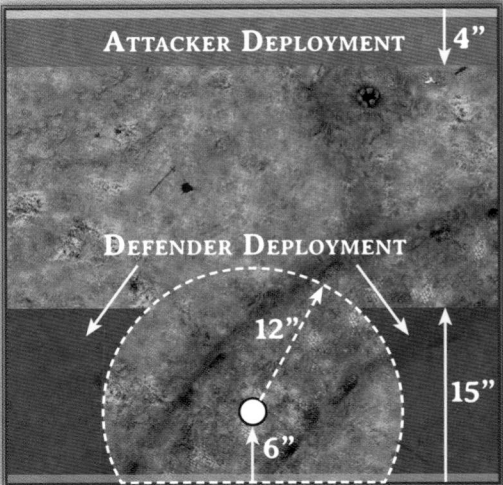

ATTACKER DEPLOYMENT 4"

DEFENDER DEPLOYMENT

12"

15"

6"

Kings of War Hook

If the Attacker wins, in their next KoW game, they may select an Infantry unit from an army list of the same alignment as their army, up to the value of 10% of the army total (e.g. in a 2000 points game, a unit up to 200 points). This unit is added to their army for free.

If the Defender wins, they may select 2 non-Hero units from the enemy army that will be delayed. These units cannot move (must make a Halt! Order) in their first turn to represent this.

3. FREE THE PRINCESS

Taken and forced into chains, the princess knows not what her fate holds. Her successful capture will be seen as a boon to the invading army and a despairing loss to her own people. Held captive at an overnight camp, can she be freed at first light to renew her people's hopes, or will she be delivered to a lifetime of servitude, torture and endless suffering?

Set-up

Roll-off to decide who will be the Attacker and who will be the Defender (with the captured princess).

Place the captured princess objective marker on the table 3" from the Defending player's table edge in the centre. The Defenders are deployed in a 9" x 18" rectangle around the princess. The Attackers approach from the opposite side of the board and can be deployed anywhere on the battlefield more than 20" from the princess.

Place 1/3 of the terrain to be used in the Attacker's half of the battlefield and the rest in the Defender's half.

The Attacker takes the first Turn in the first Round.

The Winner

The Attacking player wins if the princess is cut free and is controlled by one of their models at the end of the last Round OR she is cut free and all Defenders have been killed.

The Defending player wins if the princess remains tied up, is controlled by one of their models.

In the case of the Princess being still on the board uncontrolled, the game ends in a draw.

Scenario Rules

To interact with the princess, a standing model must be in base contact with her, not Engaged and with no enemy models in base contact with her. A model may take a long action to cut the princess free. The princess objective marker is static, blocks both movement and LOS until an action is taken to cut her free. At that point a model may control her as a free action (only the attacker may cut her free). Once controlled, place the princess marker on the card of the controlling model (or next to the model). If that model is killed

or Knocked-down, place the princess marker back on the battlefield in the footprint of the removed model or adjacent to it if Knocked down. The Defender may recapture her by moving into base contact with her when no attacking model is controlling her.

If the Princess is ever cut free and uncontrolled, at the start of each Round she will wander D8+3" towards a random board point (Roll a D8 and see map below for the corresponding location). If the Princess reaches the edge of the battlefield she will stop. At the start of the next Round, instead of rolling a die, turn the Pricess to face back into the table and move her D8+3" towards the exact centre. She will never fight, stopping 1" from any model if her move would make her engage in combat and will move around Impassable Terrain

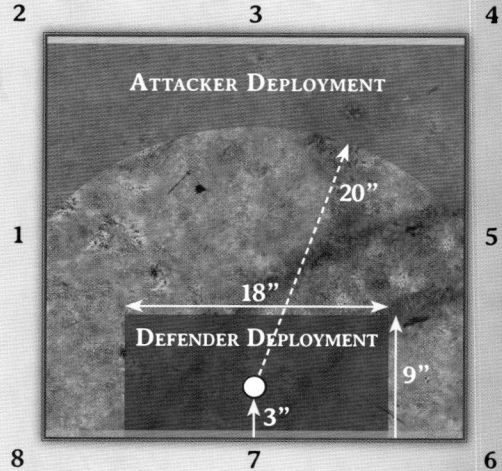

Kings of War Hook

The winner of this scenario, in their next KoW game, they may grant one unit in their army the Inspiring special rule. Nightstalker armies must instead add +2 to the Ne values of one of their units.

4. RECOVER THE PLANS

Intelligence about an opponent is key in any war. When word reaches you that an enemy spy has been cut down amidst an unexpected skirmish, the chance to retrieve the stolen battle plans must be grasped. Can the spy's comrades complete the mission and capture the plans or can the defender retrieve this vital information and keep it from the enemy?

Set up

Place a marker representing a dead spy in the exact centre of the table. Prepare an additional objective counter but don't place it yet. This will represent the possible location of the plans if they are not found on the dead spy's body. Counters should not be larger than 40mm across. The additional objective marker, if revealed during play, will be placed in one of the opposite corners of the table, 3" in from the table edges.

Concentrate some of your terrain around the two potential outlying objective locations S1 and S2, making them equally difficult to access.

Roll off to decide who will be the Attacker (trying to seize the plans) and the Defender (trying to recover their plans!). Now deploy the forces as normal, into the deployment zones in each corner as shown in the diagram.

The Winner

Both players are aiming to find the plans. The player that has a model in control of the plans at the end of the last Round is the winner.

Scenario Rules

Objective counters are static, don't block movement or LOS and cannot be moved.

When any model reaches the dead spy objective marker (base contact) for the first time, roll a die. On a 6-8 the plans are found on the dead spy. Otherwise roll another die. On a 1-4 a trail to objective marker location S1 is discovered instead. The plans had been stashed away in secret (before the spy's untimely death!). On a 5-8 a trail to objective marker location S2 is discovered instead. Place the additional objective marker on the newly discovered location – this is where the plans are.

No model may be within 3" of either of the potential objective marker locations before the dead spy objective has been searched and the plans (or trail to the hidden stash) located.

To capture the plans, a model must be in base contact with an objective marker (either the original one or a revealed one if the plans were not found on the spy), standing, not Engaged and with no enemy models in base contact with the same objective marker. A model must make a short action to claim the plans. In any other condition, the plans cannot be claimed.

Once captured, place the spy marker on the card of the controlling model. While carrying the plans, a model has a maximum Speed value of 6. If that model is killed or Knocked-down, place the spy marker back on the battlefield in the footprint of the removed model or adjacent to it if Knocked-down. The plans can be claimed from this marker by another model as described above.

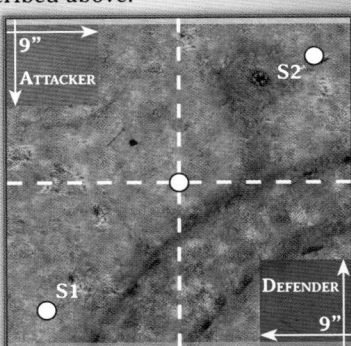

Kings of War Hook

If the Attacker wins, in their next game of KoW, they may deploy up to 3 of their units after all their opponents units have been deployed and before Vanguard moves.

If the Defender wins, they may choose to give the *Vanguard* Special Rule to up to 2 of their units AFTER both sides have deployed their model but before any Vanguard moves are taken.

5. KILL THE BARD!

Famous they said. Notorious they said. Neither was really true of the bard. He had big ideas, a bigger mouth and a fondness for talking out of turn; listening to things he should not and singing of things better left unsaid. Better dead and quiet than any further risk was what the Captain said - and you mean to see it done. It seems others have the same idea...

Set up

Place a model or marker representing the bard in the position marked on the map, 3" in from the corner.

Use a couple of buildings and some hedges, hills and some wooded areas, leaving a "road" clear for the bard to move to the opposite corner. Focus the terrain placement in the green areas as shown on the map.

Players may only deploy 50% (rounding up) of their models at the start of the game. The remaining models must enter play into their deployment zones (from an edge) as activations in Round 2.

The Winner

Both players are aiming to reach and kill the bard and then capture his lute as proof. The player with control of the lute at the end of the last Round is the winner.

Scenario Rules

At the start of each Round before any player takes a Turn, roll a die and apply the following result.

Roll	Action
1-3	Meandering poet. Move the bard 6"
4-6	Skipping along! Move the bard 12"
7-8	Awful cacophony! Move the bard 3" and mark all models within 6" of the bard as Fatigued.

The bard has the *Stealthy* and *Dodge* special rules if shot with a ranged weapon and always counts as partially obscured. The bard cannot attack but has the *Parry* special rule, and has an Armour of 5+ and 6 Wounds. The bard can break away from models without having to make any Armour Rolls and can move through any models, skipping past them as if they were not there. The bard is not affected by Difficult Terrain and only deviates from

moving directly towards the opposite corner if Impassable Terrain is encountered. The bard never takes Nerve checks, and is never marked as Activated or Fatigued. As soon as the bard reaches 0 wounds, he is killed - replace the model with a marker representing the fallen lute.

To capture the lute, a model must be in base contact with the lute marker, standing, not Engaged and with no enemy models in base contact with the lute objective. The model must make a short action to claim the lute. In any other condition, the lute cannot be claimed.

Once captured, place the lute marker on the card of the controlling model. If that model is killed or Knocked-down, place the lute marker back on the battlefield in the footprint of the removed model or adjacent to it if Knocked down.

The game immediately ends if the bard reaches the opposite corner of the battlefield where he then escapes!

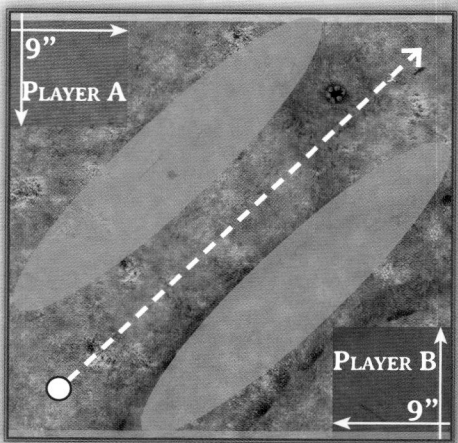

Kings of War Hook

The winning player may take the Lute of Insatiable Darkness artefact for free in their next game of KoW.

6. THE DRAGON'S EGG

A treasure rarely spoken of and even rarer held. An egg taken from the nest of a great wyrm demands an impressive price that would restock army supplies aplenty. Though it might serve other purposes too, some tales tell that such a gift can even lead its angered mother upon the battlefield to rain flame and fury!

Set up

Place a model or marker representing a dragon's egg in the position marked on the map, 6" in from the centre of an edge.

Focus the terrain placement in the green areas as shown on the map.

Players roll-off and set up in the corners marked on the map on the opposite side to the egg.

The Winner

Both players are aiming to reach and capture the egg and then carry it back to their army. The player with control of the egg at the end of the last Round is the winner. If any player has a model controlling the egg in their own deployment zone at the end of any Round, they automatically win the game.

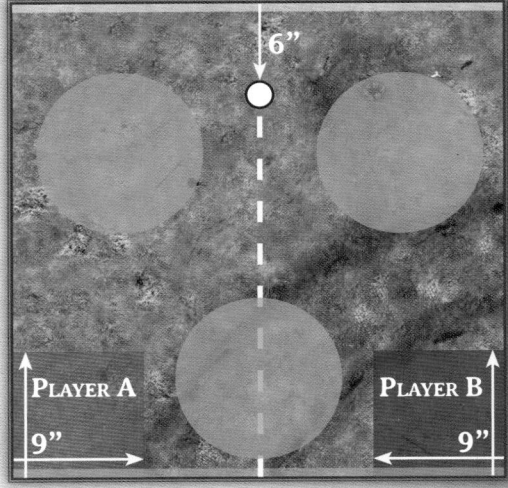

Once captured, place the egg marker on the card of the controlling model. If that model is killed or Knocked-down, place the egg marker back on the battlefield in the footprint of the removed model or adjacent to it if Knocked-down.

A model controlling the egg may only make *Walk* and *Run* actions and cannot Retaliate in a Melee. Models that are BEASTS cannot control the egg. Models carrying the egg cannot use the *Fly* special rule and may move a maximum of 12" with a single action.

At the start of each Round roll a die. On the roll of 6 or more, any model carrying the egg is attacked by an angry dragon from the skies and must make an Armour roll with a -3 modifier to avoid taking a wound and being Knocked-down!

Scenario Rules

To claim and control the egg, a model must be in base contact with the egg marker, standing, not Engaged and with no enemy models in base contact with the egg objective. The model must make a short action to claim the egg. In any other condition, the egg cannot be claimed.

Kings of War Hook

In their next game of Kings of War, the winning player may give one unit in their army the *Breath (12)* and *Piercing (1)* special rules.

7. THE POWER STONES

Mantica endures a delicate balance between the forces of nature and the abyss. Certain waypoints exist in the world, where the natural forces of magic flow more strongly through the earth. Ancient stones, carved by people's lost to the mists of time act as lodestones that can harness these currents and protect the natural balance... or destroy it.

Set up

Place 3 terrain pieces on the table to represent the power stones – these should not be larger than 40mm across. Place one in the centre of the table between the players, and the others 12" away in either direction from the central one and 4" towards the players as shown below.

Now deploy the forces using the standard set-up as described on page 48.

Power stone markers are Height 4 Impassable Terrain.

If they are within 3" of the central Power Stone at the start of a Round, COMMAND models may add an extra RED power dice to their player's pool.

While within 3" of any of the Power Stones, SPELLCASTERS may add 3" to any spell they cast that has a Range.

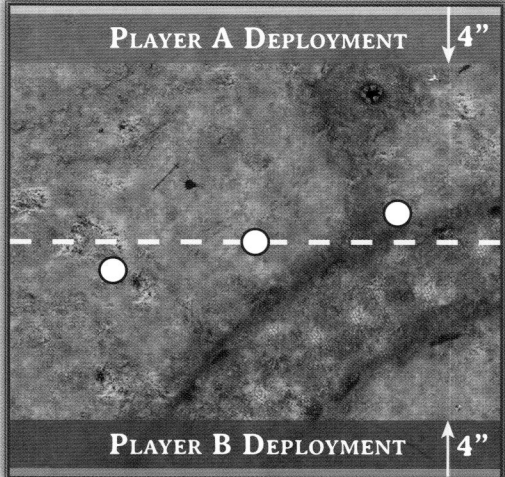

The Winner

Both players are aiming to capture the stones and tap their power. The centre one is worth 2 Victory Points (VPs). The outer ones are worth 1 VP each.

Calculate the VP scores for each side at the end of EACH ROUND. At the end of the game, sum the VPs each player scored in each Round to find the total for each player. The player with the most VPs wins.

Kings of War Hook

The winning player may give either the Heal (2) spell (Good and Neutral armies) or Lightning Bolt (2) (Evil armies) to any unit in their army. If the unit already has this spell, its n value is increased by 2 (e.g. Lightning Bolt (3) becomes (5)).

Scenario Rules

To capture a power stone, a model must be in base contact with it, standing, not Engaged and with no enemy models in base contact with the same objective. In any other condition, an objective cannot be claimed.

Alternate game

Try playing with 5 Power Stones instead of 3. Place 1 in the middle worth 3 VPs and then the players take it in turns to place the others outside deployment areas and not within 6" of another counter. These are worth 1VP each

8. CAPTURE THE GIANT!

Rumours of a fearsome mountain giant, descended from its mountain lair and terrorising the local farmsteads, have reached the ears of your scouts. Capturing and subjugating such a beast would surely be a huge boon for your forces and a terrible monster to unleash upon your foe. It's an easy job… what are you waiting for!?

Set up

Make sure you have a suitable model ready to represent the giant on a 50mm square base or even bigger.

Place the Giant in the exact centre of the table facing the 1 point on the board edge.

Now deploy the forces using the standard set-up as described on page 48.

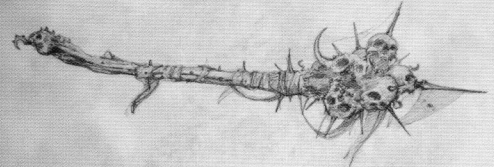

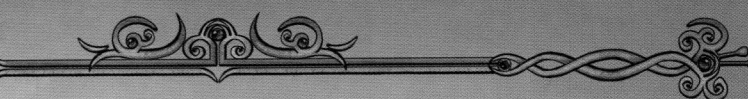

Map:

2		3		4
PLAYER A DEPLOYMENT ↓4"				
1		●		5
PLAYER B DEPLOYMENT ↑4"				
8		7		6

The Winner

Both players are aiming to capture the giant by wearing it down and tiring it out while at the same time weakening the enemy warband. At the end of each Round, the Warband which caused the most wounds on the Giant that Round, scores 3 VPs. If both Warbands cause the same number of wounds, neither score any VPs that Round. Players also score 1 VP for each enemy COMMAND, SPELLCASTER, LARGE or SUPPORT model they kill. Models that have more than one Class still only score 1 VP.

The player with the most VPs at the end of the last Round is the winner. If the totals are equal, the game is a draw.

Scenario Rules

At the start of each Round after the first, before a Turn is taken, roll a die. Turn the Giant to face the point on the table indicated on the map and move it D8+8" directly towards that point (for example, if you rolled a 4, the Giant would move 12"). The Giant isn't affected by anything other than Impassable Terrain which it will move around, taking the most direct route it can. Any model that the Giant passes through or comes within 2" of it will attack before continuing to move. Roll 6D8, hitting on 5+, with the *Crushing Strength (2)* and *Pound* special rules. Models that were Engaging the Giant at the start of the Round can be ignored and will not be attacked in this way but must each make a single Armour Roll to avoid suffering a wound as the Giant moves away.

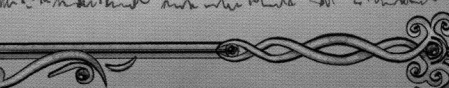

The Giant never takes Nerve checks and is never marked as Activated or Fatigued.

The Giant is largely immune to shooting. It effectively has the *Dodge* special rule and the *Piercing* value of all shooting against it is reduced by 2, to a minimum of 0.

The Giant is Height 8, has Armour 3+ and unlimited wounds. It cannot be Knocked-down and can always Break Away without making an Armour Roll. Basically, it's almost unstoppable! If the Giant reaches the edge of the battlefield it will stop. At the start of the next Round, instead of rolling a die, turn it to face back into the table and move it D8+8" towards the exact centre where it first began.

Kings of War Hook

The winning player may take a free Giant unit in its next game of KoW...even if the army doesn't have one in its list! Use the unit entry from the Ogre force list. However, the poor thing is a little wounded after its encounter with the warbands and so starts the game with D8 damage. The giant is considered an Ally but doesn't count towards the points cost limit of any Allied contingent in the army

9. DESTROY THE BAGGAGE TRAIN

All armies need a large baggage train to support their troops with food, money, tradesmen, tools, victuallers, camp followers and slaves. Not to mention the siege engines and ammunition that many armies use to batter enemy fortifications to the ground. Catching an enemy's baggage train poorly defended is an opportunity not to be missed!

Set up

Roll off to decide who will be the Attacker and the Defender.

You will need 3 model wagons or carts to represent the baggage train.

Set up your scenery, leaving a 4" wide "road" across the middle line of the table, between the two players as shown.

The Defender deploys their whole warband and the 3 wagons in the deployment zone along the road. At least 1 model must be placed in base contact with each wagon. The wagons must be further than 6" from a table edge and more than 6" from each other. The Attacker then deploys their whole warband first in the areas marked on the map, with at least 2 models in each area. Ignore the *Scout* special rule during set up.

Scenario Rules

The wagons are Height 3 Impassable Terrain and block LOS. They have 6 Wounds each and an Ar value of 4+. They have no Rear Arc. As soon as they reach 0 wounds, they are destroyed. Once destroyed, mark them as such but leave them where they are

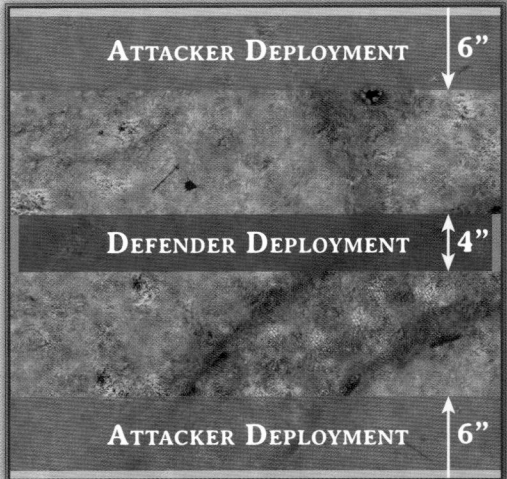

The Winner

The Attacker scores 1 VP for each wound they cause on a wagon. If all three wagons are destroyed at the end of the game, the Attacker scores an additional 2 VPs. The Defender scores 1 VP for each full 10 points of Attacking models they kill (assuming a standard 200 point game). Thus both sides can score up to 20 VPs.

The player with the most VPs at the end of the last Round is the winner. The Attacker cannot win by simply killing the defending models!

Kings of War Hook

In your next game of KoW, before deployment if the Attacking player won, they may select the cheapest (by points) value Troop unit (or Regiment if no Troops) from their opponent's army and remove them as already destroyed (which will also count towards the KoW game result) – they are not deployed. In addition, if the Attacker destroyed all three wagons, they may also remove 1 magical artefact from an enemy unit up to the value of 25 points.

10. BURN THE STORES

An army marches on its stomach. Finding and destroying your enemy's store house is as good as killing them in battle – and with less risk!

Set up

You will need some small markers to represent flames. Coins or even wound counters are sufficient.

Roll off to decide who will be the Attacker and the Defender.

Set up your scenery, placing a building representing a barn (containing the army stores), roughly 6" square in size in the position indicated on the map (B). In the other corner, place another building representing an ale house as shown on the map (A).

The Defender deploys their whole warband first. They must place 3 models in base contact with the barn to represent the guards. Two of these must be WARRIORs and/or GRUNTs. The Defender then deploys all their remaining warband models in base contact with the alehouse. They have been alerted to the danger and are on their way to help.

The Attacker now places 3 models in the deployment zone marked X on the map. Two of these must be WARRIORs and/or GRUNTs. The Attacker then deploys all their remaining warband models in the area marked Y on the map.

Ignore the *Scout* special rule during set up.

The Attacker takes the first Turn in the first Round.

The Winner

The Attacker wins if there are 4 or more Flame markers on the barn at the end of the last Round. Any other result is a win for the Defender.

Scenario Rules

The buildings are both Height 6 Impassable Terrain and block LOS.

An unengaged, standing model that is in contact with the barn may take a long action to either add a Flame marker (Attacker) onto the building, or remove an existing Flame marker (Defender). This represents the struggle between the sides to set the barn alight... or douse the flames! Keep track of the number of Flame markers on the barn with the counters next to it.

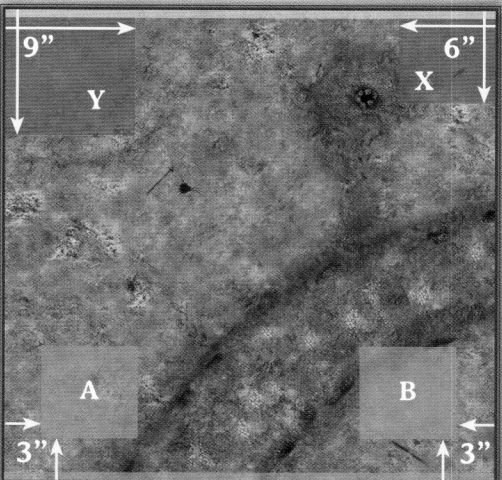

Kings of War Hook

If the Attacking player won, in their next game of KoW, they may select up 2 Infantry, Large Infantry or Cavalry units from their opponent's army. These units are suffering from the effects of reduced sustenance and poor equipment! Their Speed value is reduced by one and they suffer a -1 modifier to hit in Melee.

11. SECURE THE PORTAL

A portal to the heart of the Abyss has been opened by a mad zealot. The Abyss is a fickle mistress however and it has pulled the zealot into its depths to suffer an eternity of torment. Whether you choose to seal the portal as soon as possible or keep it open for your own nefarious purposes is up to you and your schemes...

Set up

Before placing other terrain, place a model representing the portal on a small hill in the exact middle of the table. Roll to choose deployment areas and proceed as normal.

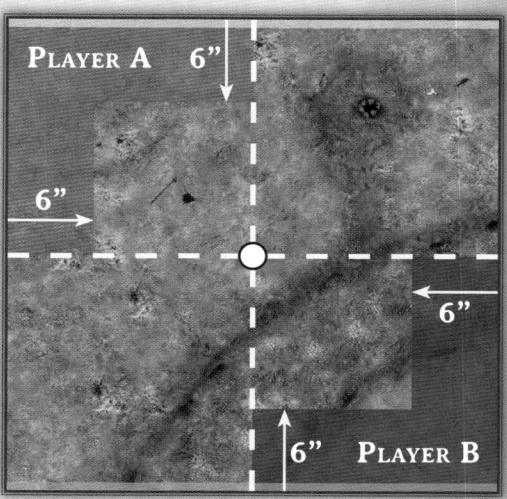

The Winner

Players can score VPs at the end of each Round and should keep a running total.

The player with the most VPs at the end of the game is the winner.

Scenario Rules

For each standing model a player has in base contact with the portal at the end of a Round, they score 1VP. If a model is a SPELLCASTER and/or COMMAND it scores 3VPs instead of 1.

After VPs have been scored and before the next Round, roll a die for each model in base contact with the portal. On a roll of 7 or 8, that model is sucked into the Abyss and counts as killed for the purposes of this scenario! In a campaign, they return to the mortal realm, deposited in a heap – roll for any injuries as normal for a "killed" model.

The portal is Height 3 Impassable Terrain and blocks LOS.

Kings of War Hook

In the next game of KoW, if the winner's KoW army alignment is Good, they may add the Elite special rule to any one unit in their army for free. If the winner's KoW army alignment is Evil, they may add the Vicious special rule to any one unit in their army for free. If their army alignment is Neutral, they may choose which of the two special rules to give a single unit If a unit already has the special rule, it may be granted the other one instead (*Elite* or *Vicious*).

The losing player finds their army cursed. In their next game of KoW, the first time the Inspiring or Very Inspiring rule would grant a re-roll on a Nerve test for one of their units, the re-roll cannot be taken and the initial result stands.

12. KILL THE COMMANDER

Everyone needs a safe place to call home, even when on campaign. Therefore, attacking an enemy in their bed has both military and psychological advantages. If you happen to find and catch the enemy commander napping, even better.

Set up

Roll off to decide who will be the Attacker and the Defender.

You will need 3 model tents to represent the campsite. Place these and a good amount of battlefield debris in the campsite area shown on the map (within 9" of the centre of the table). One tent must be placed in the exact middle of the table. No tent may be within 4" of another. Set up all other terrain outside this area as normal.

The Defender sets up first, deploying their whole warband within the campsite area. Select one of their COMMAND models to be the Commander. This model is not deployed with the rest of the warband (see scenario special rules). The Attacker then deploys their whole warband in the four corners of the map. A least one attacking model must be placed in each corner.

Both sides ignore the *Scout* special rule during set-up.

The Attacker takes the first Turn in the first Round.

The Winner

The Attacker wins if the sleeping commander is found and killed by the end of the game. The Defender wins if the sleeping commander is not killed by the end of the game.

Scenario Rules

The tents are Height 3 Impassable Terrain and block LOS.

If a standing, unengaged Attacking model is in base contact with a tent it may search it as a short action. Roll a die to make the search:

Roll	Result
1-4	Found nothing
5-6	Found battle plans
7-8	Found the sleeping commander!

Each tent may only be searched once per Round but any number of times in a game. Once the sleeping commander is found, any further result of 7-8 is treated as "Found Battle Plans". If the commander has not been found by the time the last tent is searched for the first time, the commander is automatically found. Place the now awakened commander model in 1" away from the tent and the model that found them.

The Commander may now act normally as part of the Defender's warband. Until it is awake, it does not count as being on the table and may not be used to re-roll power dice (although a second COMMAND model would still allow this).

Any table edge is a Fallback edge for BOTH sides.

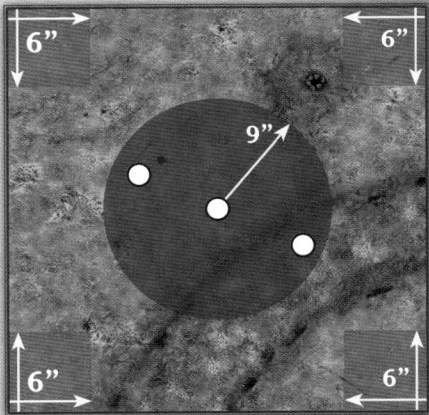

Kings of War Hook

If the Attacker wins, they may choose the table edge they wish to deploy on in their next game of Kings of War without having to roll off.

If the Attacker found the battle plans, they may choose to go first or second in the KoW game, after both sides have deployed (regardless of whether they killed the Commander or not).

BACKGROUND

Once, the world was in balance. That time is no more; it is an age recorded only in dusty scrolls or on the monuments of drowned cities. It is little more than a legend, for those who live in Mantica today remember little but war. There are, perhaps, some who remember better days – those half-gods or near-immortals gifted in sorcery – but if so, they hold their silence.

Since ancient times, the world has been ravaged by war. The wise foresee an age of horror approaching, for the spirit of the earth is sick, tainted by deadly sorcery in a great conflict ages past. Not that the warlords of this bloody era care, not while there is glory to be won, territory to be wrested from the enemy, foes to be slaughtered. The so-called Noble Peoples – Men, Elves and Dwarfs – now struggle for power and influence, battling across the ruins of long-dead realms, or staking claim to new lands. Their ancient pacts are no more. The kingdoms that pledged their armies in service of those sacred treaties are gone into legend, the descendants of the noble princes who swore eternal oaths of friendship warring openly with one another. The glorious empires of those days are lost to the ocean, or buried beneath shifting sands, the palaces of the wise now home to kraken or shambling revenants, while the scions of their great houses are exiled or long-dead.

There are but a few places where the light of the old era persists, where the remaining deities of noble intent might still be implored for aid, but ranged against such evil, what hope is there for the world?

Legions of darkness, stirred to a frenzy by the Wicked Ones, march savagely upon the myriad kingdoms of Men, the scattered Elven kindreds and the subterranean holds of the Dwarfs. Mercenaries and adventurers find fame and fortune in battle, while the servants of the Shining Ones cling to a way of life that seems almost lost. Nine hundred years after the last dark god was cast down into the Abyss, Mantica trembles once more to the marching of vast armies.

The Forces of Good

Among the noble peoples of Mantica, there is universal agreement on just one point – that the Time of Light was good. Since those ancient days, through the God War, the Time of Ice, the Winter War and the Age of Conflict, evil has spread steadily through the world, purveyed by its despicable agents. It is only the forces of good that stand in their way, who seek to stem this flow, who would see evil banished from the world and Mantica returned to a state in which goodness prevails.

Of course, even among these races there are those who are more inclined to evil, whose hearts are tainted with the allure of the darker side of things – such is its corrupting nature. Nevertheless, there are races and peoples who, as a whole, pull collectively towards the light.

The Neutral Forces

To be neutral in the world of Mantica is not merely a refusal to align oneself with this race or that, nor merely a failure to declare for the forces of good of evil. Such measures of behaviour barely exist in the frame of reference for these intriguing races, and often there are not even words for these outlooks in their vocabularies. Instead, their motivations lie in far more sweeping concepts, less vague, less prone to interpretation. In the case of the Forces of Nature, natural balance and ecological harmony are the guiding influences. For the mercenary race of Ogres it is simply a matter of coin, of the building and maintaining of certain reputations. Neutral armies can therefore be found on either side of any battle, switching allegiances at any moment based on their own private principles, and this only adds to their already intriguing nature.

The Forces of Evil

Unlike the forces of good, whose impure hearts often waver towards the allure of darkness, the forces of evil themselves are near-uniformly devoid of goodness. What little good exists in the cultures of this dark end of the spectrum is brutally hunted down and obliterated at every opportunity. These are the cruel, the malicious, and almost without exception the vile-hearted races - foul creatures beyond imagining being chief among their number.

They bring nothing but chaos and suffering to the world.

Of course, to them, these are the greatest glories of all, the sources of all their power, pleasure, and desire. Their accomplishments are ever more far reaching, and having come this far there are many in Mantica who believe they can never be stopped.

Basilea

After the events of the God War and the ruinous scouring of Winter's floods, the belligerent dwarfs had retreated underground, determined no longer to involve themselves in affairs outside their own. The elves fragmented along the lines of the shattered remains of their former glories, concerned more with their own survival than the matters of lesser races. In the face of this abandonment, men faced creatures of the Abyss, marauding orcs and goblins, and even the savage men of the steppes, alone. Humanity teetered on the brink of extinction many times over during those dark centuries, surviving by dint of sheer tenacity. Even the Shining Ones, the broken remains of their former patrons the Celestians, had become unreliable and fickle.

It was at the last, when all hope seemed lost, when the Hegemon Bolisean's armies were exhausted, surrounded and cut off by a far larger orc horde, that the balance shifted. Bolisean was alone, his guards smashed into the mud, a fresh charge of orcs pounding towards him, and his blade shattered. Slumping to his knees, Bolisean threw his head back and bellowed a plea to the lightning-streaked skies above for the Shining Ones to descend and save him and his people. In return, he offered the eternal and heartfelt fealty of him and his people to the Shining Ones as the true gods of humanity.

Whether his plea caught the fickle Shining Ones in a favourable mood by chance, or whether there was something different in his cries that moved them, none will ever know. But what happened next passed forever into legend. The spirit of Domivar himself – the son of Mescator and the hero who smote the wicked ones into the Abyss at the end of the God War, appeared before Bolisean, and asked him to repeat his oath, sealing it with his own blood in the sacred ground on which he knelt. Without thinking to pause, Bolisean sliced open his palm on the jagged end of his sword, allowing several drops to mix with the wet filth of the ground.

The reaction was instant. The rains stopped with a thundercrack of pressure and a blinding flash of lightning. As the eyes of all present adjusted in the aftermath, it was to the sight of thousands of Elohi, the winged warrior guardians of the Shining Ones, standing ready over the men of the Golden Horn. The orcs faltered, and were destroyed. The magnificent and terrible creatures overwhelmed them with violence and fury that even their savage nature could not match.

The pact had been made in blood, and on that bloody field at the edge of their protectorate, the realm of Basilea was born, Bolisean becoming the first Hegemon of this new empire of men.

Since that day, Basilea has been the last shining bastion of humanity, the centre of man's power and learning, and the upholder of the traditions of Primovantor, in whose shadow it persists.

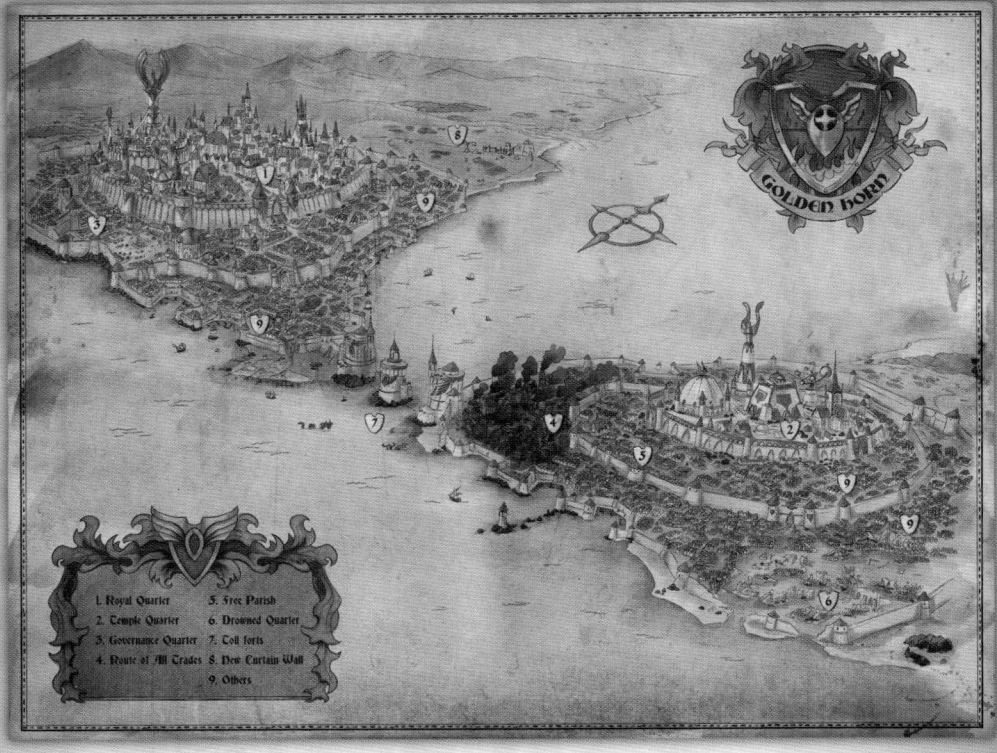

1. Royal Quarter   5. Free Parish
2. Temple Quarter   6. Drowned Quarter
3. Governance Quarter 7. Coll forts
4. Route of All Trades 8. New Curtain Wall
                      9. Others

Basilea Today

Though conservative by nature and paralysed by ritual it may be, Basilea still reflects some of the ancient glories of Primovantor. Its cities are the largest, its princes the richest, its mages the most powerful of all the kingdoms of Men. Basilea insists that it is the only true protector of Primovantor's legacy.

Temples are still maintained to the long-gone Celestians in Basilea, while the worship of their good aspects, the Shining Ones, is an integral part of life. It is a kingdom where time has stood still, where some of the glories of the elder days might still be found. Noble Paladins devote their entire lives to battle and prayer, undergoing arduous quests to prove their purity to the Shining Ones. Many Orders of the Sisterhood guard the borders. Purity, courage, and strength are the watchwords of these warrior virgins.

The Hegemon of Basilea is king and high priest both. It is within his power to appeal directly to the Shining Ones. These remaining noble aspects of the Celestians dwell atop the mountain of Kolosu, an impossibly high pillar of rock, and from there they watch over the Hegemony. They rarely manifest directly, although it is not unknown for one or the other of them to take to the battlefield even in these lesser times, but will send their servants to the aid of the Basilean armies, should the occasion warrant it. These are the Elohi, angelic beings of immense power, who appear in the guise of beautiful, winged humans armoured all in gold. In war they are all but unstoppable, as terrible in combat as they are merciful and kind out of it.

But alongside the purest aspect of true faith and benevolence, Basilea has its sinister side too. Free thinking of any kind is not easily tolerated, and Basilean culture therefore remains hidebound and unchanging. Periodic panics about agents of the Wicked Ones sweep the nation, leading to innocent and guilty alike being condemned to death by mass drowning in the Cleansing Pools. The Hegemon does not rule unchallenged; blood feud is all too common, driven by fires of honour and religious fervour that cannot be quenched. Orcs press upon Basilea from the north, while relations with the Dwarfs to the east are at their lowest ebb. And atop their pillar of stone, the Shining Ones watch, for the most part silent. Protectors of Mankind, some say, capricious immortals who toy with the lives of lesser beings, say others.

The People of Basilea

Being a people watched over by literal gods, the Basileans are both pious and conceited. It is difficult not to feel arrogant when one has beings of such power at one's back, and it is equally difficult not to have faith when your gods manifest physically before you.

The Golden Horn is full of churches, and the faith holds great temporal power. It is through the Shining Ones power and guardianship that the Hegemony has persisted these last nine hundred years, and none of its people are soon likely to forget this. Its position as a trade route and its importance as a central hub in human civilisation, combined with the reliance of smaller, satellite states on its protection, have seen Basilea grow rich and powerful. Though it may never truly rival the scale and sheer majesty of the old Primovantor, Basilea is undoubtedly one of the wealthiest nation states in all of Mantica.

The Armies of Basilea

The Basileans are adherents of the Shining Ones, and large numbers of paladins, warrior monks and battle nuns are found in their armies. The angelic Elohi fly above the hosts of Basilea, lending their pure voices to the battle hymns of holy warriors, and their strength to the army's assault.

Basilea's wealth means that its footsoldiers march to war clad in the finest plate and bearing the very best weapons that money can buy. Vast armies of them march to protect its borders, bolstered by the elite religious warriors of the Paladins on foot and atop mighty warhorses, and the fanatical sisterhood, fighting on foot or riding to battle mounted on war panthers or chariots pulled by these magnificent, if terrifying apex predators. Their warmachines are intricate and well built, and their magical support is second to none, Basilea having the highest concentration of magical colleges anywhere in the world. With these forces alone, Basilea could endure for centuries as one of the great powers of Mantica. When the forces of the Shining Ones are added, the eternal supremacy of the Golden Horn is assured. Elohi march alongside the troops of Basilea, living manifestations of divine fury, each the equal of many dozens of men. It is no surprise that Basilea has become as arrogant as it is fervent. There are simply no powers in the world who can match it. For now.

The Nightstalkers

The elven Conclave of Heaven was a secretive, intellectual project devoted to the study of higher consciousness and the nature of divinity. The pinnacle of the conclave's achievements came when it attracted the attentions of the young and seemingly curious Celestian known as Oskan. While contact was often brief and sporadic, Oskan seemed to display a bond with the elves and hinted at great changes soon to come with wonderful gifts bestowed upon the mortal world. Oskan began to teach the elven arch-mages how to travel the paths between worlds and walk in the footsteps of the gods, luring them ever further away from their bodies, testing their minds for his own amusement.

One day, the entire conclave was invited deeper into the paths, beyond the mists of time, with Oskan leading and the elves displaying an almost childish glee to see the wonders of the galaxy and other, unimaginable planes of existence. Then Elinathora smashed The Fenulian Mirror. Chaos erupted and sorcerous turmoil swept across the land and skies as the bodies of the Celestians were ripped in two. As Oskan's body was split in twain, the backwash of cosmic energy shattered the bodies, minds and spirits of the conclave around him. Acting as a conduit for this devastating surge of raw power, the mortal bodies of the elves formed the epicentre of an explosion that utterly destroyed the city where the conclave had met. The souls of the entire population and all living creatures for miles in every direction were torn from the mortal plane and scattered across countless dimensions; the screams of the victims echoing across both time and space. Feeding greedily on the minds so cruelly sacrificed, Oskan, Father of Lies, was born.

When Domivar created the Abyss with the axe of Oskan it created a rent not only in the earth but in the fabric of the universe too. The paths between realities twisted, crossed, and swelled with power. The veil between worlds grew so thin in parts that the shadow-forms of myriad, strange creatures could be seen flickering in the air, and it is the waxing and waning power of the Abyss that attracts and repels these creatures in turn. The Abyss and other sites like it across the world of Mantica are areas where reality has thinned, and such places draw things from other dimensions into the mortal world. It is here, behind fragile barriers between realities, that unimaginable things gather and lurk, desperate to find a way into the world of mortals. These are what remains of the beings horrifically torn from the world as Oskan was born. And in their absence from the mortal world they have encountered other things, too. Cosmic entities and obscene horrors who follow the shadows to the thinning veil, eying a new world to conquer; new souls to devour.

These are the Nightstalkers: the dreams, nightmares, fears and horrors of mortals become manifest. They lurk in the shadows and feed on the most powerful of mortal emotions - fear, hatred and pride. The essence of the Stalkers burrows deep into the psyche of mortals, so that each time an incursion through the veil occurs, the spirits gain a greater foothold in the world. When the power of the Abyss swells anew, those seeds that have taken root erupt violently until dark manifestations tear themselves from mortal hosts, terrorising communities, and sometimes gathering into vast hosts of unimaginable horrors. They come from shadow, sweeping through the mortal realm, taking nourishment from the very fear that precedes them. As their grip on the physical form fades, Stalkers often latch onto the bodies of the dead – or even undead – in desperation; this explains in part why shadowy spectres are so often seen in graveyards or roaming ancient battlefields. Such wretched spirits are often sought out by Necromancers, for there is much they can teach the practitioners of dark magic, if they can be successfully bound.

Cosmic Horrors

While the vast majority of the Nightstalker host comprises hollow remnants of Mantica's distant past, the things that follow them through the veil are more terrifying by far. They come from other planes, other universes – even other worlds beyond space and time. They are alien, cold and unfathomable. Their twisted forms speak to the mortals of Mantica on some primal level that few can understand. The oldest of the elves believe that these creatures serve cyclopean beings that were once gods, worshipped even before the Celestians, by cultures thankfully forgotten, or wiped out long before the elder races began to write down their history. They whisper strange names, almost unpronounceable, such as the Ch'wthall'thoi, and Tsatt'huul the fear-demon. Almost as a racial memory, these dark star-gods are still feared, such that the very sight of them can cause the weak of mind to be driven mad.

The Hosts of Shadow

Stalkers take many forms – often perceived by different races in different ways depending on the superstitions and fears of a culture or individual. As in the life they were so cruelly ripped away from, there are many different types of Stalker, sometimes even shaped by remnants of memories and personalities of their lost mortality. Sometimes, when the powers of the Abyss are strong, the presence of the Nightstalkers rips a portal in the fabric of reality – a doorway between dimensions. The power of the Abyss is channelled through such rents that seethe and boil in the air,

painful for mortals to see directly. At the edge of vision the portal seems like a cage of glossy black, writhing serpents, screaming in perpetual agony. Nightstalker shadow-hosts burst forth into reality: a gibbering, cacophonous explosion of fear wreathed in the purple lightning of the portal. The baying of spectral hounds goes before the ravenous host, while the soul-rending screams of heartless Banshees chills their foe to the bone.

Most numerous of the shadow-hosts are Spectres – hollow remnants of once-living ancients. These are the creatures that often haunt places where the dead are interred. They are mournful, skeletal creatures, wreathed in cloaks of mist and shadow. Cowardly beings, they huddle in vicious packs, lashing out at any mortal that comes near with tendrils of soul-mist. From their obfuscating presence, shambling, zombie-like Scarecrows emerge. Their presence is often heralded by wriggling swarms of bloated Blood Worms, which congregate around the Spectres' victims, sucking the blood from the dead and dying.

Manifesting from the primal fears of their enemies, blade-limbed Reapers and skull-faced Phantasms are the harbingers of the horde, whose purpose is to sow the terror required for the rest of the host to manifest. Wherever they appear, Doppelgangers are not far behind, whose mimicry of the enemy often leads to mistrust and bloody murder. And it is not merely the twisted spirits of men, Elves and Dwarfs that join the host: monstrous Stalkers also exist, such as the Shadow-hulks, seemingly fused from the souls of several giant Cyclopes and now filled with the hunger of the void.

And from the void come those emissaries of the ancient star-gods. If these creatures were ever mortal at all, it must have been some bizarre form of life that no longer exists on Mantica. Unspeakable and indescribable things, they have lived in the dimensions between worlds for an eternity. Some, like the monstrous Void Lurkers, have an intelligence of sorts and understand enough to sense the rents in the fabric of the universe and know how to locate them. They attach themselves to Nightstalkers as they stream into reality. There, they coalesce into mismatched and petrifying shapes. Other squamous horrors accompany these beasts, from vaguely arachnoid Fiends, to flickering, tenebrous Planar Apparitions.

WARBAND LISTS

Basileans

In a world beset by evil there is a single beacon of hope for the world of man. Holy crusaders and scourges of the Abyss, the resplendent forces of Basilea stride forth from their golden city to strike fear into the hearts of evildoers across the land. Their faith is as strong as their martial prowess, maintained by the pious Sisterhood and Paladin warrior-scholars in their ranks and bolstered by the dutiful Men-at-Arms and fearsome Ogre Palace Guard that march to battle alongside them.

WARBAND SPECIAL ABILITY

IRON RESOLVE (2) - This ability may be used any number of times and at any time a BASILEAN model suffers 1 or more hits. When the ability is used, the model can roll all Armour Saves at an unmodified 3+ .

FACTION SPECIFIC SPELLS

Blessed Light (long): Range 12"

Choose a friendly model within 12" of the caster. No dice roll is required. The next time that model is targeted by an attack, the attacking model must re-roll any dice that caused a hit and accept the new result.

Divine Flame (long): Range 6"

Choose a friendly model within range of the caster as the target. No dice roll is required. The target model may make a single 2D8 Melee attack at Me 3+ on an enemy model using any *Crushing Strength* the target model normally has. The enemy model may already be Engaged with the target or up to 1" away. The target model must have a Melee stat to be able to use this spell.

Boosted Version: Cost 1 Power. As above but the target model may make a second 2D8 attack in the same way against a different enemy model following the same rules.

CROSSBOWMAN				20mm		9pts
Power Dice: -			Basilean			Grunt
Sp	Me	Ra	Ar	Ne	Wn	Ht
5	6+	5+	6+	5+	1	2
Ranged: 2D8		Melee: 1D8				Good
Equipment: Crossbow: Range 12", Piercing (1), Reload						

SISTERHOOD				20mm		11pts
Power Dice: -			Basilean			Warrior
Sp	Me	Ra	Ar	Ne	Wn	Ht
5	4+	6+	6+	5+	2	2
Ranged: 1D8		Melee: 2D8				Good
Equipment: -						

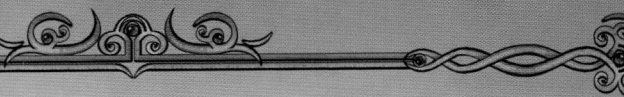

SISTERHOOD SCOUT		20mm		16pts		
Power Dice: -		Basilean		Warrior		
Sp	Me	Ra	Ar	Ne	Wn	Ht
5	6+	4+	6+	4+	2	2
Marksman, Scout						
Ranged: 2D8		Melee: 1D8		Good		
Equipment: Bow: Range 12"						

SHARP SHOOTER (1) - use this ability when this model makes a Shoot action with its Bow before any dice are rolled. Any hits are resolved with Piercing (1).

PALADIN DEFENDER		20mm		17pts		
Power Dice: -		Basilean		Warrior		
Sp	Me	Ra	Ar	Ne	Wn	Ht
5	4+	-	4+	4+	2	2
Crushing Strength (1), Defender, Parry						
Ranged: 1D8		Melee: 2D8		Good		
Equipment: -						

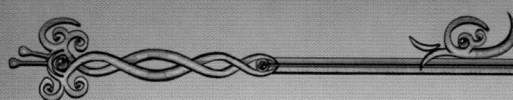

SERGEANT

		20mm		20pts		
Power Dice:		Basilean		Warrior		

Sp	Me	Ra	Ar	Ne	Wn	Ht
5	5+	5+	5+	4+	2	2

Parry

Ranged: 1D8	Melee: 2D8	Good

Equipment: -

EVADE (1) - Use this ability when the Sergeant is to perform a Break Away action. The Sergeant may Break Away from any models it is Engaged with without having to make Armour rolls and may then perform a Brace Action if desired.

GUR PANTHER

		Cav		21pts		
Power Dice: -		Basilean, Beast		Support		

Sp	Me	Ra	Ar	Ne	Wn	Ht
8	4+	-	6+	5+	3	2

Vicious

Ranged: -	Melee: 2D8	Good

Equipment: -

Reactive Bite - If this model Retaliates in Melee, it adds a bonus dice to its roll in addition to any other bonus dice or modifiers that may apply.

PALADIN CHAPLAIN

		20mm		38pts		
Power Dice: -		Basilean		Spellcaster		

Sp	Me	Ra	Ar	Ne	Wn	Ht
5	4+	4+	4+	4+	3	2

Crushing Strength (1), Defender, Parry

Ranged: 1D8	Melee: 2D8	Good

Spells: Heal (short), Shield (short), Stun (short)

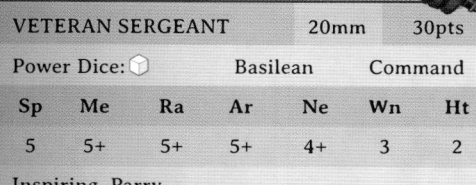

VETERAN SERGEANT

		20mm		30pts		
Power Dice:		Basilean		Command		

Sp	Me	Ra	Ar	Ne	Wn	Ht
5	5+	5+	5+	4+	3	2

Inspiring, Parry

Ranged: 1D8	Melee: 3D8	Good

Equipment: -

RALLY ON ME! (2) - This is a Group Action. The Veteran Sergeant and all members of the group may Break Away from any models they are Engaged with without having to make Armour rolls. Other models in the group must end their moves within 3" of the Veteran Sergeant. All group members then perform a Brace Action.

Dwarfs

Short in stature but as unyielding as the mountains themselves, the Dwarfs are a proud and noble people who attach a great deal of importance to heritage and custom. It is a naïve opponent indeed who does not acknowledge the Dwarf talents for war. When the Dwarfs go to war, they do so to win.

WARBAND SPECIAL ABILITY

TACTICAL REDEPLOYMENT (2) - Select a DWARF COMMAND model in the warband. All DWARF models within 9", including the nominated COMMAND model that are not knocked-down or Engaged, may immediately move up to 3" in any direction, following the normal movement rules. Models are not marked as activated after moving if they are not already. Once any moves are completed, all models that were eligible to move are given a free *Brace* action (mark them all as such).

FACTION SPECIFIC SPELLS

These spells are only available to SPELLCASTERS from the Dwarf faction. They are available to learn during a campaign (see page 144) or in one-off games (see page 122).

Earthquake (long): Range 6", Breath

Each model under the area of the *Breath* attack must roll a die. If a model rolls equal to or under its Sp stat, it is Knocked-down and must make a single Armour Roll to avoid suffering a wound. Models that have the *Steady* special rule may re-roll the test against their Sp stat.

Forged Anew (short): Range 6"

Cast on self or target a single friendly model within range, even if it is Engaged. Roll 3D8. For each 7+ rolled, the Ar stat of the target is improved by 1 until the end of the Round. (e.g. 5+ becomes 4+), to a maximum of 3+.

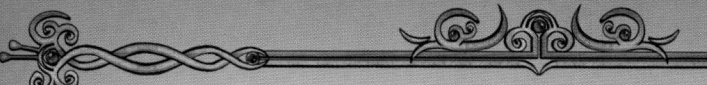

DWARF LEVY — 20mm — 8pts

Power Dice: -			Dwarf		Grunt	
Sp	Me	Ra	Ar	Ne	Wn	Ht
4	5+	5+	5+	5+	1	2

Headstrong

Ranged: 1D8	Melee: 2D8	Good

Equipment: May take a Spear for +1pt

Spear - Models with spears not Engaged with an enemy model but within 2" of a friendly model that is, grant the Engaged model one bonus die for its Melee attacks. Only 1 bonus die may be given to a model in this way, regardless of the number of spears in range. Models with spears participating in a Group Charge Action to do not have to engage enemy models but must end their move within 2" of a model in the group that is engaged.

SHIELDBREAKER — 20mm — 14pts

Power Dice: -			Dwarf		Warrior	
Sp	Me	Ra	Ar	Ne	Wn	Ht
4	4+	6+	5+	5+	2	2

Crushing Strength (1), Headstrong

Ranged: 1D8	Melee: 2D8	Good

Equipment: -

Shieldbreaker Hammer - The model may reroll one of its Melee attack dice that failed to cause a hit.

IRONCLAD — 20mm — 13pts

Power Dice: -			Dwarf		Warrior	
Sp	Me	Ra	Ar	Ne	Wn	Ht
4	4+	6+	4+	5+	2	2

Headstrong

Ranged: 1D8	Melee: 2D8	Good

Equipment: -

Hammer and Anvil - Ironclad models engaged with the same enemy model as one or more friendly Shieldbreakers, have the Swarm special rule.

IRONWATCH — 20mm — 16pts

Power Dice: -			Dwarf		Warrior	
Sp	Me	Ra	Ar	Ne	Wn	Ht
4	5+	5+	5+	5+	2	2

Headstrong

Ranged: 2D8	Melee: 1D8	Good

Equipment: Crossbow: Range 12", Piercing (1), Reload

Combined Fire - When involved in a Group Shoot Action, Ironwatch models add +1 dice to their Ranged Attack roll if one or more other Ironwatch models in the group fire at the same target.

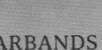
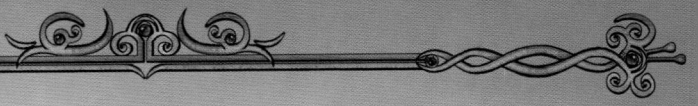

EARTH ELEMENTAL				40mm		35pts
Power Dice: -		Elemental				Large
Sp	Me	Ra	Ar	Ne	Wn	Ht
4	5+	-	4+	4+	6	3
Crushing Strength (2), Smash, Steady						
Ranged: -		Melee: 4D8			Good	
Equipment: -						

IRONGUARD				20mm		27pts
Power Dice: ⬛		Dwarf				Support
Sp	Me	Ra	Ar	Ne	Wn	Ht
4	3+	6+	4+	4+	2	2
Crushing Strength (1), Defender, Headstrong						
Ranged: 1D8		Melee: 3D8			Good	
Equipment: -						

STONE PRIEST				20mm		28pts
Power Dice: -		Dwarf				Spellcaster
Sp	Me	Ra	Ar	Ne	Wn	Ht
4	6+	4+	6+	4+	3	2
Headstrong, Inspiring						
Ranged: 1D8		Melee: 2D8			Good	
Spells: Fireball (short), Hammer (long), Heal (short)						

DWARF SERGEANT				20mm		31pts
Power Dice: ⬜		Dwarf				Command
Sp	Me	Ra	Ar	Ne	Wn	Ht
4	4+	5+	4+	5+	4	2
Crushing Strength (1), Headstrong, Inspiring						
Ranged: 1D8		Melee: 3D8			Good	
Equipment: -						

Elves

One of the oldest of the civilised races, the Elves have mastered warfare as they have every other pastime to which they turn their minds. Elves rarely take to the field in great numbers, but when they do their victory is all but assured. Mercilessly drilled infantry and uncannily accurate bowmen combine to wipe their foes from existence in short order.

WARBAND SPECIAL ABILITY

PRETERNATURAL AGILITY (3) - Until the end of the current Round, all models in the warband of race ELF, have the *Parry* and *Dodge* rules.

FACTION SPECIFIC SPELLS

These spells are only available to SPELLCASTERS from the Elf faction. They are available to learn during a campaign (see page 144) or in one-off games (see page 122).

Enchant Weapons (short): Range 12", 1D8

Target a friendly, un-activated model, even if it is Engaged. If a hit is scored, no wounds are caused. Instead, the model gains a +1 modifier to all its Melee and Ranged attack rolls in its new Turn.

Astral Mirror (long): Range 9"

Target an enemy SPELLCASTER. For the remainder of the Round, roll a die each time that SPELLCASTER casts a spell. On a 6+ the spell fails with no effect. Any action (short or long) or Power the model used is still spent. In addition, the enemy SPELLCASTER must then make an Armour roll to avoid taking a wound.

CITIZEN LEVY			20mm		8pts	
Power Dice: -			Elf		Grunt	
Sp	Me	Ra	Ar	Ne	Wn	Ht
6	5+	6+	5+	5+	1	2
Ranged: 1D8		Melee: 2D8			Good	
Equipment: -						

KINDRED ARCHER			20mm		16pts	
Power Dice: -			Elf		Warrior	
Sp	Me	Ra	Ar	Ne	Wn	Ht
6	6+	4+	5+	5+	2	2
Ranged: 2D8		Melee: 1D8			Good	
Equipment: Bow: Range 12"						

Combined Fire - When involved in a Group Shoot Action, Kindred Archer models add +1 dice to their Ranged Attack roll if one or more other Kindred Archer models in the group fire at the same target.

KINDRED TALLSPEAR — 20mm — 13pts

Power Dice: -				Elf		Warrior
Sp	Me	Ra	Ar	Ne	Wn	Ht
6	4+	6+	5+	5+	2	2

Ranged: 1D8	Melee: 2D8	Good

Equipment: Spear

Spear - Models with spears not Engaged with an enemy model but within 2" of a friendly model that is, grant the Engaged model one bonus die for its Melee attacks. Only 1 bonus die may be given to a model in this way, regardless of the number of spears in range. Models with spears participating in a Group Charge Action to do not have to engage enemy models but must end their move within 2" of a model in the group that is engaged.

KINDRED GLADESTALKER — 20mm — 26pts

Power Dice: -				Elf		Support
Sp	Me	Ra	Ar	Ne	Wn	Ht
6	4+	4+	6+	5+	2	2

Marksman, Pathfinder, Scout

Ranged: 2D8	Melee: 2D8	Good

Equipment: Bow: Range 12"

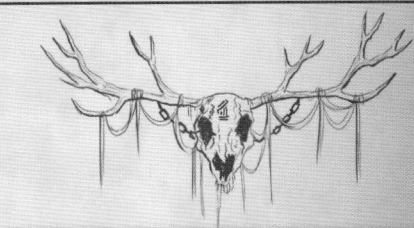

BATTLE-CAT — Cav — 17pts

Power Dice: -			Beast		Support	
Sp	Me	Ra	Ar	Ne	Wn	Ht
7	5+	-	6+	5+	2	2

Bloodlust

Ranged: -	Melee: 3D8	Good

Equipment: -

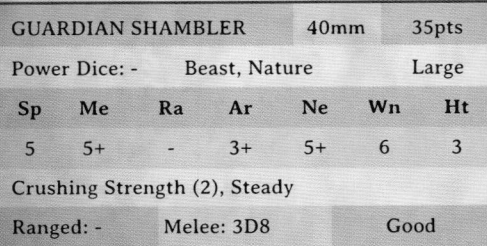

GUARDIAN SHAMBLER — 40mm — 35pts

Power Dice: -		Beast, Nature				Large
Sp	Me	Ra	Ar	Ne	Wn	Ht
5	5+	-	3+	5+	6	3

Crushing Strength (2), Steady

Ranged: -	Melee: 3D8	Good

Equipment: -

PROTECT (n) - Pay (n) Power, up to the number of wounds the Guardian Shambler has left, to transfer any wounds just caused on a single friendly ELF model within 3" onto the Shambler instead. Reduce the Shambler's wounds accordingly and remove it if it is reduced to zero. This ability can be used at any time.

BATTLE-MAGE				20mm		38pts
Power Dice:				Elf		Spellcaster
Sp	**Me**	**Ra**	**Ar**	**Ne**	**Wn**	**Ht**
6	5+	4+	6+	4+	3	2

Ranged: 1D8	Melee: 2D8		Good

Spells: Heal (short), Lightning Bolt (long),
Mind Storm (long)

RANGE BOOST (2) - Use this ability to increase the
range of one of the caster's spells by 6" (where a Range
is specified). The RANGE BOOST must be paid for
during the caster's activation just before the chosen
spell is cast.

PRINCE				20mm		44pts
Power Dice:				Elf		Command
Sp	**Me**	**Ra**	**Ar**	**Ne**	**Wn**	**Ht**
6	3+	4+	4+	4+	4	2

6th Sense, Crushing Strength (1), Inspiring

Ranged: 2D8	Melee: 4D8		Good

Equipment: -

BATTLE RAGE (2) - If this model can Engage an enemy
model with a follow-up move, it may Engage that model
and initiate another Melee by using the ability to go
into a Battle Rage. This model will not get any bonus
dice for charging however. Once this second Melee has
been resolved, mark this model as Fatigued.

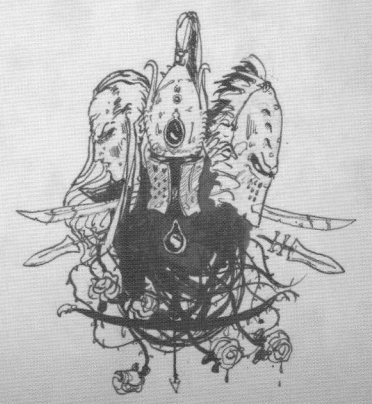

 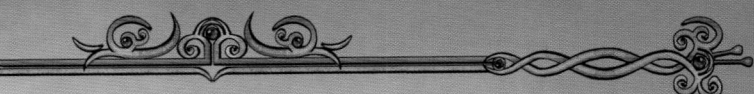

Northern Alliance

In the frozen wastes of the Winterlands, the Northern Alliance has carved out a fledgling empire, quite literally from the ice and rock of a bleak and unforgiving wilderness. The exiled prince, Talannar, has assembled a formidable and eclectic mix of the dispossessed and disenfranchised, uniting them under a common banner and goal. For what purpose though, outsiders can only speculate, for little news or rumour spills from the icy grip of Talannar's fortress city of Chill.

WARBAND SPECIAL ABILITY

HARDY VETERANS (1) - Use this ability when a model would be Knocked-down, Spend 1 power to gain the *Steady* special rule for this attack. Models that already have *Steady* may re-roll the result.

Talannar's Pack - Northern Alliance Warbands may take 1 additional LARGE model than the game size would normally allow.

FACTION SPECIFIC SPELLS

These spells are only available to SPELLCASTERS from the Northern Aliance faction. They are available to learn during a campaign (see page 144) or in one-off games (see page 122).

Hold Fast (short): Range 9"

Target a friendly model, even if it is Engaged. For the remainder of the Round, that model has a +1 modifier to any Nerve tests it is required to make and may add 1 bonus die to any Armour rolls it must take.

Boosted version: Cast as a long action instead. As above, but the modifier is increased to +2 and the bonus dice are increased to 2.

Winter's Bite (long): Range 12", 3D8

If the target suffers any wounds, they are Knocked-down and marked as Fatigued.

DWARF CLANSMAN				20mm		8pts
Power Dice: -			Dwarf		Grunt	
Sp	Me	Ra	Ar	Ne	Wn	Ht
4	5+	5+	5+	5+	1	2
Headstrong						
Ranged: 1D8	Melee: 2D8				Good	
Equipment: May take a Frosthammer for +1pt						

Frosthammer - A great two-handed hammer wielded by the Dwarf clans in the North. The model gains Crushing Strength (1) but increases its Ar by 1 (i.e. 5+ to 6+).

HUMAN CLANSMAN				20mm		8pts
Power Dice: -			Human		Grunt	
Sp	Me	Ra	Ar	Ne	Wn	Ht
5	5+	5+	5+	5+	1	2
Ranged: 1D8	Melee: 2D8				Good	
Equipment: -						

HUSCARL				25mm		15pts
Power Dice: -			Human		Warrior	
Sp	Me	Ra	Ar	Ne	Wn	Ht
5	5+	5+	4+	4+	2	2
Crushing Strength (1)						
Ranged: 1D8	Melee: 3D8				Good	
Equipment: -						

ICE NAIAD				20mm		12pts
Power Dice: -			Neritican		Warrior	
Sp	Me	Ra	Ar	Ne	Wn	Ht
6	5+	5+	6+	5+	2	2
Regenerate (7+)						
Ranged: 1D8		Melee: 2D8			Good	
Equipment: Frost-Trident						

Frost-Trident - For any wound caused by a Melee attack with the Frost-Trident, the target model is pinned in place until the end of their next activation. While the model is pinned their Sp is reduced to 0 and they cannot make a Break Away action.

HALF-ELF BERSERKER				20mm		19pts
Power Dice: -			Half-elf		Warrior	
Sp	Me	Ra	Ar	Ne	Wn	Ht
6	4+	-	6+	4+	2	2
Bloodlust						
Ranged: -		Melee: 3D8			Good	
Equipment: -						

FRENZY (1) - Use this ability to gain 2 bonus dice when this model makes a Melee attack (not a Retaliation). Spend the power before rolling any dice. Cannot be used in conjunction with the normal use of Power to gain a bonus dice for a roll.

ICE KIN HUNTER — 20mm — 26pts

Power Dice: -			Elf		Support	
Sp	Me	Ra	Ar	Ne	Wn	Ht
6	5+	4+	6+	4+	2	2

Marksman, Pathfinder, Scout

Ranged: 2D8	Melee: 1D8	Good

Equipment: Bow: Range 12"

RAPID FIRE (2) - Use this ability when this model is about to perform a ranged attack, before dice are rolled. The model may shoot twice at two different targets that are within 3" of each other following the normal targeting rules. This cannot be as part of a Group or Fatigue Action.

SNOW TROLL — 40mm — 34pts

Power Dice: -			Troll		Large	
Sp	Me	Ra	Ar	Ne	Wn	Ht
6	5+	-	4+	4+	5	3

Crushing Strength (2), Regenerate (6+), Vicious

Ranged: -	Melee: 4D8	Good

Equipment: -

Vicious Swipe - When attempting to Break Away from a Troll, enemy models have a -1 modifier when they make their Armour Save roll.

SNOW TROLL PRIME — 40mm — 54pts

Power Dice: ⬡			Troll		Large, Command	
Sp	Me	Ra	Ar	Ne	Wn	Ht
6	4+	-	4+	3+	5	3

Crushing Strength (2), Regenerate (6+), Vicious

Ranged: -	Melee: 5D8	Good

Equipment: -

Vicious Swipe - When attempting to Break Away from a Troll, enemy models have a -1 modifier when they make their Armour Save roll.

Forces of Nature

When the balance of the world is truly threatened, the Druids call upon all manner of creatures to protect it. From the vicious Salamanders to the lumbering Forest Shamblers, all answer the call. The ground shakes and the forests heave as the Forces of Nature march to war.

WARBAND SPECIAL ABILITY

FOREST DWELLERS (1) - Until the end of the current Round, all models in this warband have the *Pathfinder* rule.

AMBUSH (1) - During any Turn, when an enemy model comes within 3" of the terrain piece nominated for your Lurker model, or enters it, you can use this ability to place your ambushing (Lurker) model into play within 3" of the enemy model. If the enemy model enters the terrain, the ambushing model may be placed in contact with it, Engaged, in its front arc. The ambushing model is marked as Fatigued but may be activated as normal later in the Round. The enemy model immediately ends its current action but may continue its Turn.

Lurker - During deployment, you may elect to place ONE of your SUPPORT models in ambush in any piece of Difficult Terrain (not Impassable) outside of your opponent's deployment area. Make a note of which terrain piece you are choosing and put the model to one side of the table. This model is a Lurker.

FACTION SPECIFIC SPELLS

These spells are only available to SPELLCASTERS from the Forces of Nature faction. They are available to learn during a campaign (see page 144) or in one-off games (see page 122).

Barrier of Vines (long)

Place a 1"x 6" marker anywhere within 12" of the caster, into Open Ground and clear of any models. The area described by the marker is Height 10 Impassable Terrain and blocks LOS. In the End Phase of each Round roll a die. On a 5+, the barrier is removed. The casting model can only have one such barrier in play at any time.

Vengeful Flock (long): Range 6"

A blizzard of furious birds is summoned. Target a single enemy model within 6". All models within 2" of the target may suffer the effects of this attack as follows. Roll 1D8: on a roll of 1-4 all models suffer a 2D8 6+ Melee attack; on a 5-6 all models suffer a 2D8 5+ Melee attack; on a 7-8 the the original target model takes the full fury of the flock and suffers a 3D8 3+ Melee attack. In addition, if the model survives it is picked up and moved 6" in a direction of the casting player's choice, and is then placed Knocked-down and Fatigued. The model cannot be placed in Impassable Terrain or within 1" of another model.

SALAMANDER UNBLOODED		25mm		11pts		
Power Dice: -		Salamander				Grunt
Sp	Me	Ra	Ar	Ne	Wn	Ht
5	4+	-	5+	6+	2	2
Crushing Strength (1)						
Ranged: -		Melee: 2D8			Neutral	
Equipment: -						

CENTAUR BRAY-STRIDER			Cav		22pts	
Power Dice: -			Nature			Warrior
Sp	Me	Ra	Ar	Ne	Wn	Ht
7	3+	-	5+	5+	2	3
Cavalry, Smash						
Ranged: -		Melee: 2D8			Neutral	
Equipment: -						

NAIAD — 20mm — 12pts

Power Dice: -		Neritican			Warrior	
Sp	Me	Ra	Ar	Ne	Wn	Ht
6	5+	5+	6+	5+	2	2

Regenerate (7+)

Ranged: 1D8	Melee: 2D8	Neutral

Equipment: Trident. May take a Harpoon-gun for +3pts

Trident - For any hit scored with this weapon the target model is automatically Fatigued.

Harpoon-gun - Range 9", Piercing (1)

NAIAD ENSNARER — 20mm — 17pts

Power Dice: -		Neritican			Support	
Sp	Me	Ra	Ar	Ne	Wn	Ht
6	5+	5+	6+	5+	2	2

Regenerate (7+)

Ranged: 1D8	Melee: 2D8	Neutral

Equipment: Trident, Net

Trident - For any hit scored with this weapon the target model is automatically Fatigued.

Net - Break away actions from this model are made rolling 2 dice for the armour roll rather than the normal 1. Each failed roll causes a wound as normal.

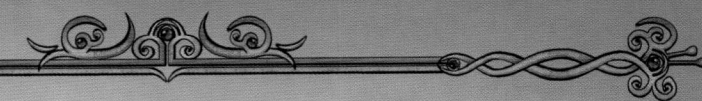

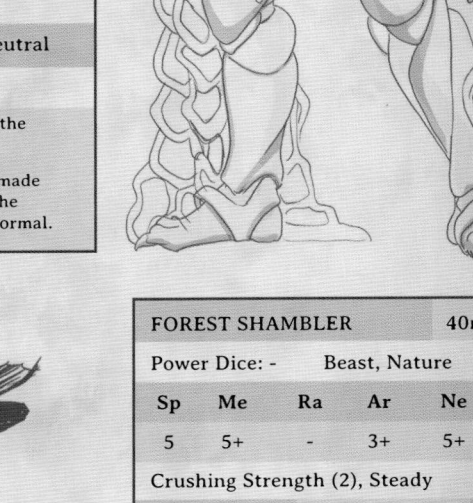

FOREST SHAMBLER — 40mm — 33pts

Power Dice: -		Beast, Nature			Large	
Sp	Me	Ra	Ar	Ne	Wn	Ht
5	5+	-	3+	5+	6	3

Crushing Strength (2), Steady

Ranged: -	Melee: 3D8	Neutral

Equipment: -

WILD COMPANION — 20mm — 17pts

Power Dice: -		Beast, Nature			Support	
Sp	Me	Ra	Ar	Ne	Wn	Ht
7	5+	-	6+	5+	2	2

Pathfinder

Ranged: -	Melee: 2D8	Neutral

Equipment: -

HIS MASTER'S VOICE (1) - Use this ability to activate up to two friendly Wild Companion models within 3" of a friendly COMMAND or SPELLCASTER Class model. The activations are taken at the same time but the models may complete their activation independently (this is not a group activation). This can be performed in addition to the normal +1 model activation if bought with Power.

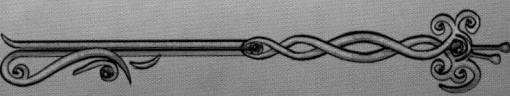

DRUID			20mm		36pts	
Power Dice: 🎲			Nature		Spellcaster	
Sp	Me	Ra	Ar	Ne	Wn	Ht
5	5+	4+	6+	4+	3	2
Inspiring						
Ranged: 1D8		Melee: 2D8			Neutral	

Spells: Heal (short), Lightning Bolt (long),
Windblast (long)

RANGE BOOST (2) - Use this ability to increase the
range of one of the caster's spells by 6" (where a Range
is specified). The RANGE BOOST must be paid for
during the caster's activation just before the chosen
spell is cast.

CENTAUR CHIEF			Cav		45pts	
Power Dice: 🎲			Nature		Command	
Sp	Me	Ra	Ar	Ne	Wn	Ht
8	3+	4+	5+	4+	4	3
Cavalry, Smash						
Ranged: 2D8		Melee: 3D8			Neutral	
Equipment: Bow: Range 12"						

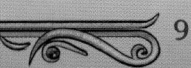

Ogres

Ogres are mercenaries, happy to sell their skills to the highest bidder. Huge, powerful creatures that might almost have been purpose bred for war, few races can match them for sheer belligerent power and endurance, and many a war has been won by the side that hired the most. When Ogres do unite into larger Companies, it is a rare thing indeed. There is no record of an army ever holding fast against them and scholars debate long into the night as to whether this is because Ogres have so rarely united in force, or because no opposition has ever survived to tell the tale.

WARBAND SPECIAL ABILITY

BRUTAL ROAR (1) - Use this ability when an OGRE model charges. When the model becomes engaged, the target must make a Nerve test. If it fails, place a Fatigue counter on it.

High & Mighty - An Ogre Warband (or Company) has no limits on the number of LARGE OGRE models it can have. The normal limit still applies to any other LARGE models the warband might take.

FACTION SPECIFIC SPELLS

These spells are only available to SPELLCASTERS from the Ogre faction. They are available to learn during a campaign (see page 144) or in one-off games (see page 122).

Battle Fury (long): Range: 9"

Target a friendly model that is not Knocked-down or Engaged. No dice roll is required. That model may immediately make a *Melee* action for free against any model it is Engaged with, even if it is already Activated and/or Fatigued.

Might of the Tribes (long): Range 9"

Target a friendly model, even if it is Engaged. That model may re-roll any failed Armour rolls until the end of the Round. In addition, the *Crushing Strength* and *Piercing* special rules are limited to (1) against this model unti the end of the Round.

BRAVE					40mm	17pts
Power Dice: -				Ogre	Large, Grunt	
Sp	Me	Ra	Ar	Ne	Wn	Ht
6	5+	-	5+	5+	3	3
Crushing Strength (1)						
Ranged: -		Melee: 3D8			Neutral	
Equipment: -						

Body Guard - Ogre Brave models have a +1 modifier to their Melee attacks while within 6" of a friendly Ogre Warlock.

RED GOBLIN RABBLE				20mm		7pts
Power Dice: -			Goblin			Grunt
Sp	Me	Ra	Ar	Ne	Wn	Ht
5	5+	7+	5+	6+	1	2
Sneaky						
Ranged: 1D8		Melee: 1D8			Neutral	

Equipment: May take a Spear for +1pt

Spear - Models with spears not Engaged with an enemy model but within 2" of a friendly model that is, grant the Engaged model one bonus die for its Melee attacks. Only 1 bonus die may be given to a model in this way, regardless of the number of spears in range. Models with spears participating in a Group Charge Action to do not have to engage enemy models but must end their move within 2" of a model in the group that is engaged.

OGRE WARRIOR				40mm		23pts
Power Dice: -			Ogre		Large, Warrior	
Sp	Me	Ra	Ar	Ne	Wn	Ht
6	4+	-	5+	5+	3	3
Crushing Strength (1)						
Ranged: -		Melee: 4D8			Neutral	
Equipment: -						

SIEGE BREAKER — 40mm — 34pts

Power Dice: -		Ogre		Large, Support		
Sp	Me	Ra	Ar	Ne	Wn	Ht
5	4+	-	4+	5+	4	3

Crushing Strength (3), Smash

Ranged: -	Melee: 4D8	Neutral

Equipment: -

BOOMER — 40mm — 40pts

Power Dice: -		Ogre		Large, Support		
Sp	Me	Ra	Ar	Ne	Wn	Ht
6	6+	5+	5+	5+	3	3

Crushing Strength (1)

Ranged: 1D8	Melee: 2D8	Neutral

Equipment: Boomer: Range: 9", 4D8, Piercing (1), Area Effect (3" / 2D8 / Piercing (1), Reload)

RED GOBLIN BIGGIT — 20mm — 23pts

Power Dice: ▣		Goblin		Support		
Sp	Me	Ra	Ar	Ne	Wn	Ht
5	5+	5+	5+	5+	3	2

Crushing Strength (1), Inspiring (Goblin models only), Sneaky

Ranged: 2D8	Melee: 3D8	Neutral

Equipment: -

OGRE WARLOCK — 40mm — 36pts

Power Dice: ▣		Ogre		Large, Spellcaster		
Sp	Me	Ra	Ar	Ne	Wn	Ht
6	5+	5+	5+	5+	3	3

Ranged: 3D8	Melee: 2D8	Neutral

Spells: Fireball (short), Tribal Assault (short), Windblast (long)

CACKLE! (1) - Use when the model activates. The model may cast the same spell twice this Turn if it has enough actions.

TRIBAL ASSAULT (1) - Use this ability as a spell. Choose an enemy model within 9" and LOS of the Warlock. The chosen model must roll 2D8, plus one extra dice for each friendly Brave within 6" of the Warlock. If any dice roll an 8, the target takes one wound with no armour roll possible.

OGRE CAPTAIN — 40mm — 48pts

Power Dice: ▣		Ogre		Large, Command		
Sp	Me	Ra	Ar	Ne	Wn	Ht
5	3+	-	4+	5+	5	3

Crushing Strength (2), Headstrong, Vicious

Ranged: -	Melee: 4D8	Neutral

Equipment: -

DEFENSIVE SLAM (2) - Use this ability when the Captain attacks a model in Melee. That model cannot Retaliate against any Melee attacks made by the Captain this Turn.

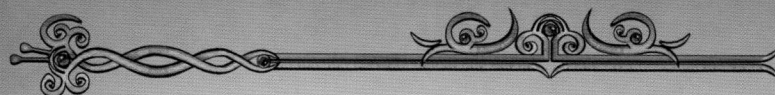

The Trident Realm

The Kingdoms of the Trident Realm are proud and territorial, and can commit to violence with little provocation. The lord of any land-bound territory would be wise to treat their inlets and coasts cautiously, lest they stir the fierce Neriticans who claim them as their own. When the Trident Realm stirs, the very seas boil – storms rage, waves crash upon coastlines and the tides rise only to retreat, revealing the Neritican host, water cascading off shells and armour and ready for war.

WARBAND SPECIAL ABILITY

RISING TIDES (2) - Use this ability at the start of a Turn. Until the end of the Round, all models in the warband of Race NERITICAN increase their Speed stat by 2 when making any basic *Walk* or *Run* movement action (climbing is excluded). Alternatively, instead of gaining the extra Speed, any NERITICAN model that is Knocked-down can perform a *Stand Up* action for free when they are activated. This ability may only be used once per Turn.

FACTION SPECIFIC SPELLS

These spells are only available to SPELLCASTERS from the Trident Realm faction. They are available to learn during a campaign (see page 144) or in one-off games (see page 122).

Crushing Pressure (long): Range: 6", 3D8, Piercing (1)

If the target suffers any wounds, they are pinned in place and cannot make any *Walk* or *Run* actions for the rest of this Round.

Riptide (long): Range 9"

Target up to two enemy models within 3" of each other, even if they are Engaged. Targeted models are moved 3" (as directly and as far as possible) away from the caster, making Armour rolls if forced to *Break Away* as normal. Any models that were moved are then Knocked-down. Models with the *Steady* special rules are only Knocked down on a 5+ on a single die roll.

OTTER BEVY			40mm	10pts
Power Dice: -	Beast, Neritican			Grunt
Sp	Me	Ra	Ar	Ne	Wn	Ht
6	4+	-	7+	7+	3	1
Swarm, Vicious
Ranged: -	Melee: 2D8		Neutral
Equipment: -

THUUL			20mm	12pts
Power Dice: -	Neritican			Warrior
Sp	Me	Ra	Ar	Ne	Wn	Ht
5	3+	7+	6+	5+	2	2
Ranged: -	Melee: 2D8		Neutral
Equipment: -

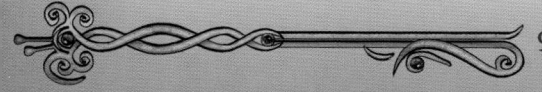

NAIAD HEARTPIERCER				20mm		14pts
Power Dice: -			Neritican			Warrior
Sp	Me	Ra	Ar	Ne	Wn	Ht
6	5+	5+	6+	5+	2	2
Regenerate (7+)						
Ranged: 2D8		Melee: 1D8			Neutral	
Equipment: Harpoon-gun: Range 9", Piercing (1)						

RIVERGUARD				20mm		14pts
Power Dice: -			Neritican			Warrior
Sp	Me	Ra	Ar	Ne	Wn	Ht
6	6+	5+	6+	6+	2	2
Pathfinder, Vicious						
Ranged: 2D8		Melee: 1D8			Neutral	
Equipment: Javelin: Range 9", Pound						

BOUNDER (1) - Use this ability when this model is activated. Grants this model the Fly ability until the end of the Round.

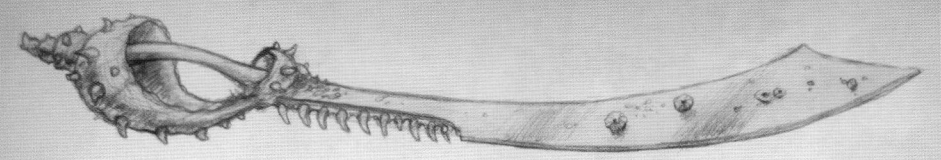

THUUL MYTHICAN				20mm		26pts
Power Dice: 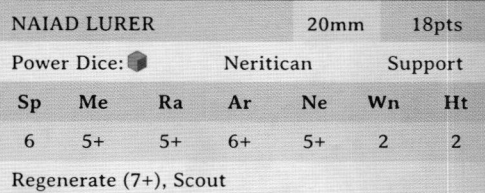		Neritican			Spellcaster	
Sp	Me	Ra	Ar	Ne	Wn	Ht
5	5+	5+	6+	5+	2	2
Inspiring						
Ranged: 1D8		Melee: 2D8			Neutral	

Spells: Shockwave (long), Stun (short), Windblast (long)

NAIAD LURER				20mm		18pts
Power Dice:		Neritican			Support	
Sp	Me	Ra	Ar	Ne	Wn	Ht
6	5+	5+	6+	5+	2	2
Regenerate (7+), Scout						
Ranged: 1D8		Melee: 2D8			Neutral	

Equipment: Trident, Net

Trident - For any hit scored with this weapon the target model is automatically Fatigued.

Net - Break away actions from this model are made rolling 2 dice for the armour roll rather than the normal 1. Each failed roll causes a wound as normal.

WATER ELEMENTAL				40mm		32pts
Power Dice: -		Elemental			Large	
Sp	Me	Ra	Ar	Ne	Wn	Ht
6	5+	-	4+	4+	4	3
Crushing Strength (2), Regenerate (6+)						
Ranged: -		Melee: 5D8			Neutral	

Equipment: -

NAIAD CENTURION				20mm		45pts
Power Dice:		Neritican			Command	
Sp	Me	Ra	Ar	Ne	Wn	Ht
6	4+	4+	5+	4+	3	2
Crushing Strength (1), Inspiring, Regenerate (7+)						
Ranged: 2D8		Melee: 4D8			Neutral	

Equipment: Harpoon-gun: Range 9", Piercing (1)

BATTLE RAGE (2) - If this model can Engage an enemy model with a follow-up move, it may Engage that model and initiate another Melee by using the ability to go into a Battle Rage. This model will not get any bonus dice for charging however. Once this second Melee has been resolved, mark this model as Fatigued.

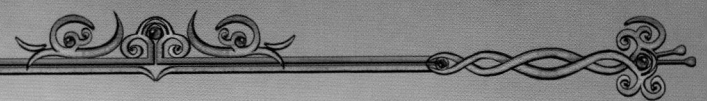

Abyssal Dwarfs

Twisted, evil parodies of their mountain-dwelling brethren. The Abyssal Dwarfs make use of slaves to bolster their numbers, and dark technologies to rain fire and destruction on their foes.

When the hordes of Tragar march forth, the world trembles before them. The ground shudders under the march of thousands of slaves and soldiers, and the air shivers with the sound of arcane weaponry and dark sorcery.

WARBAND SPECIAL ABILITY

SLAVEHOOKS (X) - Use this ability when activating an un-Engaged, standing, ABYSSAL DWARF model in this warband. Make a free Ranged attack with the activating model with Range 6", (X+1)D8, *Piercing (1)*, where X is the amount of Power used. If the attack causes any wounds on the target enemy model, it must roll 1D8. If the result is greater than the Speed of the model (or a natural 8), mark it as Fatigued. For example, if 2 Power were used, the number of dice rolled would be (2+1)D8 = 3D8 dice in total.

FACTION SPECIFIC SPELLS

These spells are only available to SPELLCASTERS from the Abyssal Dwarf faction. They are available to learn during a campaign (see page 144) or in one-off games (see page 122).

Iron Slam (long): Range: 9", 3D8, Crushing Strength (n)

If any hits are scored, the target is picked up and slammed into the ground. The *Crushing Strength* of the attack is equivalent to the number of hits scored. For example, if 2 hits are scored, the hits have *Crushing Strength (2)*. If any wounds are suffered, the target is Knocked-down.

Slave to the Flame (long): Range 6"

The target suffers 1 automatic hit with *Crushing Strength (3)*. If the model is not killed, it MUST be the first model in its Warband to activate in the following Round. If multiple models must act first before any others, the owning player may choose the order they are activated. Mark the casting model as Fatigued.

SLAVE ORC				25mm		11pts
Power Dice: -				Orc		Grunt
Sp	Me	Ra	Ar	Ne	Wn	Ht
5	5+	7+	5+	6+	2	2
Crushing Strength (1)						
Ranged: 1D8	Melee: 2D8					Evil
Equipment: -						

Stay in Line! - While within 3" of a friendly Slave Driver model, a Slave Orc automatically passes all Nerve tests.

BLACKSOUL				20mm		14pts
Power Dice: -		Abyssal Dwarf				Warrior
Sp	Me	Ra	Ar	Ne	Wn	Ht
4	4+	6+	4+	5+	2	2
Vicious						
Ranged: 1D8	Melee: 3D8					Evil
Equipment: -						

Hammer and Anvil - Blacksoul models engaged with the same enemy model as one or more friendly Immortal Guard have the Swarm special rule.

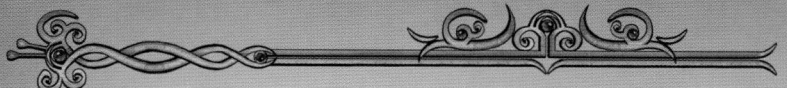

ABYSSAL HALFBREED			Cav		24pts	
Power Dice: -			Beast		Warrior	
Sp	Me	Ra	Ar	Ne	Wn	Ht
6	4+	6+	4+	5+	2	3
Cavalry, Smash, Vicious						
Ranged: 1D8		Melee: 3D8			Evil	
Equipment: -						

DECIMATOR			20mm		21pts	
Power Dice: -		Abyssal Dwarf			Warrior	
Sp	Me	Ra	Ar	Ne	Wn	Ht
4	5+	5+	5+	5+	2	2
Vicious						
Ranged: 2D8		Melee: 1D8			Evil	
Equipment: Blunderbuss: Range 9", Breath, Piercing (1), Reload						

GARGOYLE — 25mm — 18pts

Power Dice: -		Abyssal			Support	
Sp	Me	Ra	Ar	Ne	Wn	Ht
7	5+	-	6+	6+	2	2

Fly, Regenerate (4+), Vicious

Ranged: -	Melee: 2D8	Evil

Equipment: -

MOBILE KATSUCHAN — 20mm — 34pts

Power Dice: -		Abyssal Dwarf			Support	
Sp	Me	Ra	Ar	Ne	Wn	Ht
4	5+	5+	5+	5+	2	2

Vicious

Ranged: 1D8	Melee: 1D8	Evil

Equipment: Rocket Launcher: Range 9", 3D8, Piercing (1), Reload, Area Effect (2" / 1D8)

LESSER OBSIDIAN GOLEM — 50mm — 37pts

Power Dice: -		Elemental			Large	
Sp	Me	Ra	Ar	Ne	Wn	Ht
4	5+	-	4+	4+	4	3

Crushing Strength (3), Smash, Steady

Ranged: -	Melee: 5D8	Evil

Equipment: -

HARD AS NAILS (2) - Use this ability when the Golem fails any Armour Rolls. Re-roll all the dice that failed. Any that score a 5+ will save a wound (note that exploding 8s do not apply to any dice re-rolled using this ability).

SLAVE DRIVER — 20mm — 34pts

Power Dice: ⬡		Abyssal Dwarf			Command	
Sp	Me	Ra	Ar	Ne	Wn	Ht
4	4+	5+	5+	5+	3	2

Inspiring, Vicious

Ranged: 1D8	Melee: 3D8	Evil

Equipment: -

Slavers Whip - Roll (X+2)D8 when using the SLAVEHOOKS warband ability with this model. In addition, the target model will be Fatigued on a 4+, regardless of its Speed stat.

Forces of the Abyss

The Abyss is a strange other-realm, populated by wicked creatures locked in an eternal battle with each other. Whenever they are directed to fight the outside world, it is a time of woe for all civilised races, for the Abyssals recognise no allies.

Mass incursions of the forces of the Abyss are thankfully rare, for when they do happen, the suffering is terrible. Pouring forth in waves of demonic creatures on foot and in the air, an Abyssal horde may only ever be stopped at great cost and after much bloodshed.

WARBAND SPECIAL ABILITY

FURY (1) – Use the ability when an ABYSSAL model Retaliates in a Melee. The ABYSSAL model gets 2 bonus dice to attack. This special action may even be used on a model that is already Activated and Fatigued, allowing them to Retaliate as normal, but without the additional 2 bonus dice. This Special Ability may be used any number of times in a Round.

FACTION SPECIFIC SPELLS

These spells are only available to SPELLCASTERS from the Forces of the Abyss faction. They are available to learn during a campaign (see page 144) or in one-off games (see page 122).

Torment (short): Range: 6"

The target must make 2 Nerve tests. For each test that is failed, the target suffers a wound with no Armour roll possible.

Immolation (long): Range 6"

The target suffers 1 automatic hit. If a wound is caused, the target suffers another automatic hit as the flames continue to burn. Repeat this process until the target is either dead or the flames are put out by a successful Armour roll.

IMPS			40mm	13pts
Power Dice: -		Abyssal		Grunt
Sp	Me	Ra	Ar	Ne	Wn	Ht
6	5+	-	7+	6+	3	1
Stubborn, Swarm, Vicious						
Ranged: -		Melee: 3D8		Evil		
Equipment: -						

LOWER ABYSSAL			20mm	8pts
Power Dice: -		Abyssal		Grunt
Sp	Me	Ra	Ar	Ne	Wn	Ht
5	5+	-	5+	5+	1	2
Ranged: -		Melee: 2D8		Evil		
Equipment: -						

FLAMEBEARER			20mm		9pts	
Power Dice: -			Abyssal		Grunt	
Sp	Me	Ra	Ar	Ne	Wn	Ht
5	7+	5+	6+	5+	1	2

Ranged: 2D8	Melee: 1D8	Evil

Equipment: -

Firebolt - This model has a ranged attack with Range 9" and Piercing (1).

LEAPING FIREBOLT (1) - Use this ability when this model makes a ranged attack with Firebolt. Spend 1 power to boost the range of the attack by a further 3" (from 9" to 12"). The boosted attack remains at Piercing (1).

ABYSSAL GUARD			20mm		14pts	
Power Dice: -			Abyssal		Warrior	
Sp	Me	Ra	Ar	Ne	Wn	Ht
5	4+	-	4+	5+	2	2

Crushing Strength (1), Regenerate (6+)

Ranged: -	Melee: 2D8	Evil

Equipment: -

GARGOYLE				25mm		18pts
Power Dice: -			Abyssal		Support	
Sp	Me	Ra	Ar	Ne	Wn	Ht
7	5+	-	6+	6+	2	2
Fly, Regenerate (4+), Vicious						
Ranged: -		Melee: 2D8			Evil	
Equipment: -						

SUCCUBUS LURKER				20mm		24pts
Power Dice: -			Abyssal		Support	
Sp	Me	Ra	Ar	Ne	Wn	Ht
6	4+	-	6+	4+	2	2
Scout, Sneaky, Stealthy, Vicious						
Ranged: -		Melee: 3D8			Evil	
Equipment: -						

Fatal Attraction - While within 3" of one or more models in a warband with this rule, enemy models suffer a -1 modifier on their Melee attacks.

HELLEQUIN			Cav		29pts	
Power Dice: -			Abyssal		Support	
Sp	Me	Ra	Ar	Ne	Wn	Ht
7	3+	-	4+	4+	3	3
6th Sense, Cavalry, Crushing Strength (1)						
Ranged: -		Melee: 3D8			Evil	
Equipment: -						

HELLEQUIN BLOOD-MASQUE			Cav		42pts	
Power Dice: 			Abyssal		Command	
Sp	Me	Ra	Ar	Ne	Wn	Ht
7	3+	-	4+	4+	4	3
6th Sense, Cavalry, Crushing Strength (2)						
Ranged: -		Melee: 3D8			Evil	
Equipment: -						

Expert Rider - This model can also claim the +1 Melee attack modifier for its Cavalry special rule against targets of equal Height, not just those of lower Height.

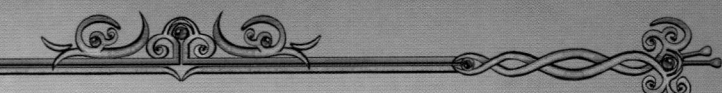

Empire of Dust

An ancient empire punished for its hubris and fall into chaos. The peoples of the Ahmunites are now a nightmare that haunt the parched, unforgiving lands of the south. Stripped of their power and life by the Ophidians and cursed for all time, the Ahmunite empire wages a vengeful war on both the living and dead alike. Fuelled by hatred and compelled by sinister necromancy, the ranks of the Ahmunites march relentlessly across the scorched earth.

WARBAND SPECIAL ABILITY

Entomb - During deployment, up to half of your warband's models (rounding up) with this special rule may be set aside and declared to be waiting in ambush under the ground. These *Entombed* models can only arrive using the Attack From Below special ability. Any models that fail to arrive by the end of the game are casualties (killed).

ATTACK FROM BELOW (X) - Use this ability once during any of your Turns. For each Power you spend, you can place one curently *Entombed* model anywhere in Open Terrain within 9" of a friendly Empire of Dust (Emp. of Dust) COMMAND model (this cannot be a model that was itself *Entombed* and set up this Round) and more than 3" away from any enemy models. Models set up this way are marked as Activated. You may still activate other models as normal. This ability is not limited to once per Round (just once per Turn).

Deathless Bond - Unlike a normal warband, an Empire of Dust warband is not Broken once it has less than half its models remaining. Instead, when the last COMMAND model in an Empire of Dust warband is killed, the warband is Broken, regardless of the number of models it has remaining.

Back from the Grave - While the warband is not broken, all standing UNDEAD models within 6" of a friendly COMMAND model, including GRUNTS, that are reduced to zero (or fewer) wounds, automatically get a Down But Not Out result. UNDEAD models attacked in Melee when already Knocked-down, are removed as normal if reduced to zero (or fewer) wounds.

Once the warband is broken however, all UNDEAD models that are reduced to zero (or fewer) wounds, automatically get a Too Much Damage result.

FACTION SPECIFIC SPELLS

These spells are only available to SPELLCASTERS from the Empire of Dust faction. They are available to learn during a campaign (see page 144) or in one-off games (see page 122).

Weakness (long): Range 9", 2D8

If any hits are scored, instead of suffering a wound, the model may roll a maximum of 2D8 (including any bonus dice) for any Ranged or Melee attack it makes until the end of the Round.

Boosted version: Costs 1 Power. As above, but in addition, any hits will halve the target's Sp stat (rounding down) and it may not use the *Crushing Strength* special rule if it has it, until the end of the Round.

Sand Storm (long): Range 12", 3D8, Piercing (1)

If the target suffers any wounds, they are marked as Fatigued.

SKELETON			20mm		6pts	
Power Dice: -		Undead, Emp. of Dust			Grunt	
Sp	Me	Ra	Ar	Ne	Wn	Ht
4	5+	6+	5+	6+	1	2
Entomb						
Ranged: -		Melee: 1D8		Evil		
Equipment: -						

SKELETON ARCHER			20mm		7pts	
Power Dice: -		Undead, Emp. of Dust			Grunt	
Sp	Me	Ra	Ar	Ne	Wn	Ht
4	6+	6+	6+	6+	1	2
Entomb						
Ranged: 1D8		Melee: 1D8		Evil		
Equipment: Bow: Range 12"						

DESERT SWARM			40mm		10pts	
Power Dice: -		Emp. of Dust, Beast			Grunt	
Sp	Me	Ra	Ar	Ne	Wn	Ht
6	7+	-	7+	4+	2	1
Swarm, Vicious						
Ranged: -		Melee: 2D8		Evil		
Equipment: -						

THEY'RE INSIDE MY ARMOUR! (2) - You may use this ability when the Desert Swarm attacks a model in Melee and gets one or more hits. The target cannot make an Armour Rolls to save against these hits.

REVENANT			20mm		10pts	
Power Dice: -		Undead, Emp. of Dust			Warrior	
Sp	Me	Ra	Ar	Ne	Wn	Ht
4	5+	-	4+	6+	2	2
Entomb						
Ranged: -		Melee: 2D8		Evil		
Equipment: -						

ENSLAVED GUARDIAN			40mm		44pts	
Power Dice: -		Emp. of Dust			Large, Spellcaster	
Sp	Me	Ra	Ar	Ne	Wn	Ht
5	5+	6+	4+	4+	5	3
Crushing Strength (2), Parry						
Ranged: -		Melee: 5D8		Evil		
Spells: Windblast (long)						

Djinn Unleashed - When this model is killed, all other models within 3" (friend and foe!) must make an Armour roll to avoid suffering a wound.

SAND WRAITH			20mm		23pts	
Power Dice: -		Undead, Emp. of Dust			Support	
Sp	Me	Ra	Ar	Ne	Wn	Ht
6	4+	-	4+	5+	2	2
Crushing Strength (1), Entomb, Fly, Stealthy						
Ranged: -		Melee: 2D8		Evil		
Equipment: -						

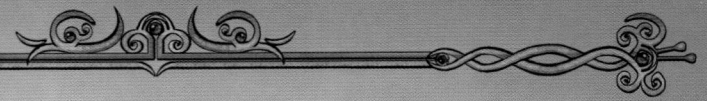

REVENANT CHAMPION		20mm		26pts		

Power Dice: 🎲 Undead, Emp. of Dust Support

Sp	Me	Ra	Ar	Ne	Wn	Ht
4	4+	-	4+	5+	3	2

Crushing Strength (1), Entomb

Ranged: -	Melee: 3D8	Evil

Equipment: -

Directed Effort - Other Emp.of Dust Skeletons and Revenants in this warband add +1 bonus die to their Range and Melee attack rolls while involved in any type of Group Action with the Revenant Champion.

PHAROAH'S CHAMPION		20mm		48pts		

Power Dice: 🎲🎲 Undead, Emp. of Dust Command

Sp	Me	Ra	Ar	Ne	Wn	Ht
5	3+	5+	4+	4+	4	2

Crushing Strength (2), Inspiring, Regenerate (6+)

Ranged: 1D8	Melee: 4D8	Evil

Equipment: -

CURSE (1) - You may use this ability when an enemy model that inflicts one or more unsaved wounds on the Pharoah's Champion. The enemy model is marked as Cursed until the end of the Round. Cursed models suffer a -1 penalty on all their attack, armour and nerve rolls. This is not cumulative with other sources of Curse but is with other applicable modifiers.

Goblins

Small, unpleasant and spiteful, Goblins are often written off by those who know no better as simply the weaker serving class of the Orc race. In fact, Goblins are utterly separate from Orcs, being not only smaller and less imposing but also far cleverer and more dexterous. They might not beat you in a straight fight, but to underestimate even a small force of Goblins would be a grave mistake.

WARBAND SPECIAL ABILITY

FLEE! (1) - When an enemy model declares the intention to Engage a GOBLIN model, the GOBLIN model may elect to Flee unless it is already activated, Fatigued or Engaged. If the GOBLIN elects to FLEE, it moves before, and directly away from, the enemy model as far as possible up to its Speed following the normal movement rules. It is then marked as Fatigued. If the enemy model can no longer reach the GOBLIN to Engage it, it may perform a *Walk* action (if it hasn't already) and then its activation is over. This special ability is not limited to one use per Round.

FACTION SPECIFIC SPELLS

These spells are only available to SPELLCASTERS from the Gobin faction. They are available to learn during a campaign (see page 144) or in one-off games (see page 122).

Slink (short): Range 6", 1D8

Target a friendly, model with a -1 modifier on the roll. If a hit is scored, instead of suffering a wound, the target model removes any Activation counter on it and can be activated again this Round in a later Turn.

Shrivel (short): Range 9", 2D8

For each hit scored, the target suffers a -1 modifier to any Melee or Ranged attack it makes until the end of the Round.

Boosted version: Cast as a long action instead. The spell rolls 3D8 rather than 2D8.

RABBLE					20mm	8pts
Power Dice: -			Goblin			Grunt
Sp	Me	Ra	Ar	Ne	Wn	Ht
5	5+	7+	5+	6+	1	2
Sneaky, Swarm						
Ranged: 1D8		Melee: 1D8				Evil
Equipment: May take a Spear for +1pt						

Spear - Models with spears not Engaged with an enemy model but within 2" of a friendly model that is, grant the Engaged model one bonus die for its Melee attacks. Only 1 bonus die may be given to a model in this way, regardless of the number of spears in range. Models with spears participating in a Group Charge Action to do not have to engage enemy models but must end their move within 2" of a model in the group that is engaged.

SPITTER			20mm		8pts	
Power Dice: -			Goblin		Grunt	
Sp	Me	Ra	Ar	Ne	Wn	Ht
5	6+	6+	6+	6+	1	2
Scout						
Ranged: 2D8		Melee: 1D8			Evil	
Equipment: Bow: Range 12"						

LUGGIT			20mm		10pts	
Power Dice: -			Goblin		Warrior	
Sp	Me	Ra	Ar	Ne	Wn	Ht
5	5+	6+	5+	6+	2	2
Sneaky						
Ranged: 1D8		Melee: 2D8			Evil	
Equipment: -						

MAWBEAST			20mm		19pts	
Power Dice: -			Beast		Support	
Sp	Me	Ra	Ar	Ne	Wn	Ht
7	5+	-	6+	5+	2	2
Vicious						
Ranged: -		Melee: 3D8			Evil	
Equipment: -						

HOWL! (1) - Use when the model activates or after it has finished its actions. Any friendly, non-Fatigued and non-activated Mawbeasts within 6" of this model can immediately make a Walk action directly towards this model without being marked as activated. An individual Mawbeast can only Howl! once per Round.

TROLL				40mm		34pts
Power Dice: -			Troll			Large
Sp	Me	Ra	Ar	Ne	Wn	Ht
6	5+	-	4+	4+	4	3
Crushing Strength (2), Pound, Regenerate (6+)						
Ranged: -		Melee: 5D8			Evil	
Equipment: -						

Vicious Swipe - When attempting to Break Away from a Troll, enemy models have a -1 modifier when they make their Armour Save roll.

WIZ				20mm		29pts
Power Dice: 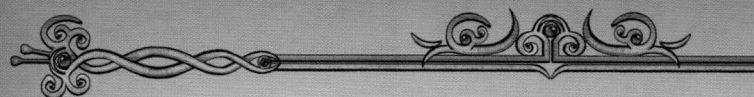			Goblin			Spellcaster
Sp	Me	Ra	Ar	Ne	Wn	Ht
5	6+	5+	6+	3+	3	2
Inspiring						
Ranged: 1D8		Melee: 1D8			Evil	

Spells: Stun (short), Zap (short)

CACKLE! (1) - Use when the model activates. The model may cast the same spell twice this Turn if it has enough actions.

BANGGIT				20mm		28pts
Power Dice: -			Goblin			Support
Sp	Me	Ra	Ar	Ne	Wn	Ht
6	6+	5+	6+	5+	2	2
Dodge, Sneaky						
Ranged: 2D8		Melee: 1D8			Evil	

Equipment: Dodgy Grenades: Range 6", Piercing (2), Area Effect (2" / 1D8)

Dodgy Grenades - When making a ranged attack, first roll 1D8. On the roll of 1, the grenande fails to explode and no further dice are rolled. Otherwise, the attack proceeds as normal.

BIGGIT				20mm		37pts
Power Dice: ◯ ◼			Goblin			Command
Sp	Me	Ra	Ar	Ne	Wn	Ht
5	4+	5+	5+	5+	3	2
Crushing Strength (1), Inspiring, Sneaky						
Ranged: 2D8		Melee: 3D8			Evil	
Equipment: -						

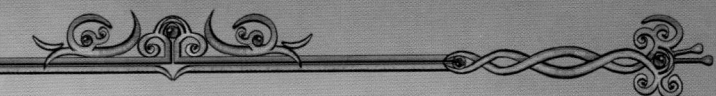
Nightstalkers

The Nightstalkers are the dreams, nightmares, fears and horrors of mortals become manifest. They lurk in the shadows and feed on the most powerful of mortal emotions - fear, hatred and pride. Nightstalker shadow-hosts burst forth into reality: a gibbering, cacophonous explosion of fear wreathed in the purple lightning of the portal. The baying of spectral hounds goes before the ravenous host, while the soul-rending screams of heartless Banshees chills their foe to the bone.

WARBAND SPECIAL ABILITY

DREAD (1) - Nominate any one of your Nightstalker models on the table that is not Fatigued. Pick one enemy model within 3" of the nominated Nightstalker. This model must immediately make a Nerve test with a -1 modifier. If the test if failed the model is marked as Activated. Any rules that apply to Nerve tests (e.g. *Inspiring*) can be used normally. This ability may be used once in each Nightstalker Turn, and is not limited to one use per Round.

FACTION SPECIFIC SPELLS

These spells are only available to SPELLCASTERS from the Nightstalker faction. They are available to learn during a campaign (see page 144) or in one-off games (see page 122).

Horrify (short): Range 6"

No dice roll is necessary and LOS is not required to the target. The target model must immediately make a Fallback Check with a -1 modifier.

Boosted version: Cast as a long action instead. As above, but the modifier is increased to -2 and a failure cannot be re-rolled for any reason.

Fear the Darkness (long): Range 12", 1D8

LOS to the target is not required. If a hit is scored, instead of taking any wounds, the target is marked as both Activated and Fatigued and must then make a Nerve test. If it is failed, the target is Knocked-down.

NEEDLEFANGS				40mm		11pts
Power Dice: -		Nightstalker			Grunt	
Sp	Me	Ra	Ar	Ne	Wn	Ht
6	5+	-	6+	4+	2	1
Bloodlust, Stealthy, Swarm						
Ranged: -		Melee: 2D8			Evil	
Equipment: -						

SCARECROW				20mm		8pts
Power Dice: -		Nightstalker			Grunt	
Sp	Me	Ra	Ar	Ne	Wn	Ht
5	6+	-	6+	4+	1	2
Mob Assault, Stealthy						
Ranged: -		Melee: 1D8			Evil	
Equipment: -						

PHANTOM				20mm		14pts
Power Dice: -		Nightstalker			Warrior	
Sp	Me	Ra	Ar	Ne	Wn	Ht
5	5+	-	5+	4+	2	2
Fly, Stealthy, Vicious						
Ranged: -		Melee: 2D8			Evil	
Equipment: -						

HORROR				20mm		12pts
Power Dice: -		Nightstalker			Warrior	
Sp	Me	Ra	Ar	Ne	Wn	Ht
5	6+	-	4+	4+	2	2
Stealthy						
Ranged: -		Melee: 2D8			Evil	
Equipment: -						

Bane Chant - Friendly NIGHTSTALKER models (but not the model itself) have the Vicious special rule while within 6" of this model.

REAPER			20mm		16pts	
Power Dice: -		Nightstalker			Warrior	
Sp	Me	Ra	Ar	Ne	Wn	Ht
5	5+	-	5+	3+	2	2
Crushing Strength (1), Stealthy						
Ranged: -		Melee: 3D8			Evil	
Equipment: -						

SHADOWHOUND			Cav		22pts	
Power Dice: -		Beast, Nightstalker			Support	
Sp	Me	Ra	Ar	Ne	Wn	Ht
7	5+	-	5+	4+	3	2
Bloodlust, Regenerate (6+), Stealthy						
Ranged: -		Melee: 2D8			Evil	
Equipment: -						

BUTCHER			40mm		33pts	
Power Dice: -		Nightstalker			Large	
Sp	Me	Ra	Ar	Ne	Wn	Ht
6	5+	-	4+	3+	4	3
Crushing Strength (2), Pound, Stealthy						
Ranged: -		Melee: 4D8			Evil	
Equipment: -						

REAPER SOULDRINKER			20mm		25pts	
Power Dice: 🎲		Nightstalker			Command	
Sp	Me	Ra	Ar	Ne	Wn	Ht
5	5+	-	4+	3+	2	2
Crushing Strength (1), Stealthy						
Ranged: -		Melee: 2D8			Evil	
Equipment: -						

Soul Thirst (short) - Use as an action. Friendly NIGHTSTALKER models (but not the model itself), while within 6" of this model, gain 1 bonus die for any Melee attack they make until the end of the current Round.

Orcs

Orcs live for war in a quite literal sense, having been bred for that very purpose by the machinations of an evil god. Over the centuries, they have developed neither culture nor civilisation, busy as they are locked in eternal battle with anything in reach, including each other. Orcs thankfully spend so much time fighting each other that they rarely gather in enough force to truly threaten the civilised races of the world. When such a gathering does occur though, it is nigh unstoppable.

WARBAND SPECIAL ABILITY

GREEN TIDE (2) - *Group Charge* Action. Until the end of the Turn, all members of the group of Race ORC gain *Crushing Strength (1)* or increase their *Crushing Strength* by one if they already have this special rule.

FACTION SPECIFIC SPELLS

These spells are only available to SPELLCASTERS from the Orc faction. They are available to learn during a campaign (see page 144) or in one-off games (see page 122).

Green Rage (short): Range 12", 1D8

Target a single friendly, non-Fatigued, un-Activated and un-Engaged model. If a hit is scored, the model suffers no wounds but must make an immediate *Run* move to Engage an enemy model. A free Melee attack will be granted for a qualifying *Charge* Action as normal. Resolve the attack as normal and then mark the model that Ran as Fatigued (not Activated) before continuing with the caster's Turn. If an enemy model cannot be Engaged, the target model will *Walk* towards the closest enemy model instead.

God-fuel (long)

Roll 4D8. For each 6+ rolled, remove a Fatigue counter from a friendly model within 6" of the caster. The caster is then marked as Fatigued.

ORCLINGS			40mm	10pts		
Power Dice: -		Orcling		Grunt		
Sp	Me	Ra	Ar	Ne	Wn	Ht
6	4+	-	7+	7+	2	1
Swarm, Vicious						
Ranged: -		Melee: 2D8		Evil		
Equipment: -						

AX			25mm	12pts		
Power Dice: -		Orc		Grunt		
Sp	Me	Ra	Ar	Ne	Wn	Ht
5	4+	7+	5+	5+	2	2
Crushing Strength (1)						
Ranged: 1D8		Melee: 2D8		Evil		
Equipment: -						

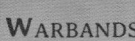

MORAX

			25mm		22pts	
Power Dice: -			Orc		Warrior	

Sp	Me	Ra	Ar	Ne	Wn	Ht
5	3+	-	7+	4+	3	2

Crushing Strength (1), Vicious

Ranged: -	Melee: 3D8		Evil

Equipment: -

FRENZY (1) - Use this ability to gain 2 bonus dice when this model makes a Melee attack (not a Retaliation). Spend the power before rolling any dice. Cannot be used in conjunction with the normal use of Power to gain a bonus dice for a roll.

GORE RIDER

			Cav		24pts	
Power Dice: -			Orc		Support	

Sp	Me	Ra	Ar	Ne	Wn	Ht
7	4+	-	5+	5+	2	3

Cavalry, Crushing Strength (1), Smash

Ranged: -	Melee: 3D8		Evil

Equipment: -

GORE (1) - Use this ability when making a Melee attack with this model. The model has the Bloodlust special rule until the end of its Turn. However, it gains 2 bonus dice instead of 1 if the target model is already wounded.

GREATAX

			25mm		16pts	
Power Dice: -			Orc		Warrior	

Sp	Me	Ra	Ar	Ne	Wn	Ht
5	4+	7+	6+	5+	2	2

Crushing Strength (2)

Ranged: 1D8	Melee: 3D8		Evil

Equipment: -

TROLL

			40mm		34pts	
Power Dice: -			Troll		Large	

Sp	Me	Ra	Ar	Ne	Wn	Ht
6	5+	-	4+	4+	4	3

Crushing Strength (2), Pound, Regenerate (6+)

Ranged: -	Melee: 5D8		Evil

Equipment: -

Vicious Swipe - When attempting to Break Away from a Troll, enemy models have a -1 modifier when they make their Armour Save roll.

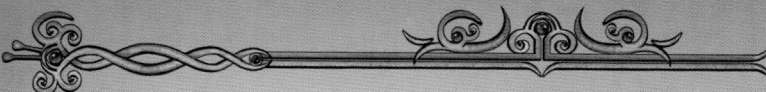

GOD SPEAKER				25mm		28pts
Power Dice: -				Orc		Spellcaster
Sp	Me	Ra	Ar	Ne	Wn	Ht
5	5+	4+	6+	4+	3	2
Headstrong						
Ranged: 1D8		Melee: 2D8				Evil

Spells: Fireball (short), Mind Storm (long)

KRUDGER				25mm		45pts
Power Dice: ▦ ▦ ▦				Orc		Command
Sp	Me	Ra	Ar	Ne	Wn	Ht
5	3+	7+	4+	4+	4	2
Crushing Strength (1), Inspiring, Stubborn, Vicious						
Ranged: 1D8		Melee: 4D8				Evil

Equipment: -

SAVAGE (1) - If the Krudger fails to kill a model in Melee, the enemy model is Knocked-down. Use the ability after armour rolls are made. Cannot be used on LARGE models.

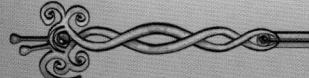   

Undead

The dead do not rest easy in Mantica, for there are those who would use them as macabre puppets to fulfil their own mortal ends. Skeletal foot troops and cavalry shamble onwards in a relentless tide, overwhelming any who stand in their path.

Even the bravest of men will blanch in terror at the sight of an Undead horde. Legions of foulness advance in horrifying silence, destroying all that they see before them without mercy or restraint. And then, the greatest horror of all, the recently dead rise up on the invisible strings of their necromantic masters to turn on those they called friends and comrades.

WARBAND SPECIAL ABILITY

SURGE (2) - Nominate a model with the COMMAND type in the Undead warband. All friendly undead WARRIOR and GRUNT models within 9" of the nominated COMMAND model may immediately make a free *Walk* action, even if they have already activated this Round or are Fatigued.

Deathless Bond - Unlike a normal warband, an Undead warband is not Broken once it has less than half its models remaining. Instead, when the last COMMAND model in an Undead warband is killed, the warband is Broken, regardless of the number of models it has remaining.

Back from the Grave - While the warband is not broken, all standing UNDEAD models within 6" of a friendly COMMAND model, including GRUNTS, that are reduced to zero (or fewer) wounds, automatically get a Down But Not Out result. UNDEAD models attacked in Melee when already Knocked-down, are removed as normal if reduced to zero (or fewer) wounds.

Once the warband is broken however, all UNDEAD models that are reduced to zero (or fewer) wounds, automatically get a Too Much Damage result.

FACTION SPECIFIC SPELLS

These spells are only available to SPELLCASTERS from the Undead faction. They are available to learn during a campaign (see page 144) or in one-off games (see page 122).

Curse of Ages (long)

No dice roll required. Until the end of the Round, all enemy models within 6" of the caster suffer a -1 modifier to all their Melee and Ranged attacks. Mark the caster as Fatigued.

Ectoplasmic Blast (long): Range 9", 1D8, Breath, Piercing (1)

GHOUL				20mm		9pts
Power Dice: -			Undead			Grunt
Sp	Me	Ra	Ar	Ne	Wn	Ht
6	5+	-	6+	4+	1	2
Dodge						
Ranged: -		Melee: 2D8				Evil
Equipment: -						

ZOMBIE				20mm		6pts
Power Dice: -			Undead			Grunt
Sp	Me	Ra	Ar	Ne	Wn	Ht
4	6+	-	7+	6+	1	2
Mob Assault						
Ranged: -		Melee: 1D8			Evil	
Equipment: -						

SKELETON				20mm		6pts
Power Dice: -			Undead			Grunt
Sp	Me	Ra	Ar	Ne	Wn	Ht
4	6+	-	5+	6+	1	2
Ranged: -		Melee: 1D8			Evil	
Equipment: -						

SKELETAL DOG PACK			40mm		9pts	
Power Dice: -		Beast, Undead			Grunt	
Sp	Me	Ra	Ar	Ne	Wn	Ht
5	6+	-	5+	6+	2	2
Swarm, Vicious						
Ranged: -		Melee: 2D8		Evil		
Equipment: -						

REVENANT			20mm		10pts	
Power Dice: -		Undead			Warrior	
Sp	Me	Ra	Ar	Ne	Wn	Ht
4	5+	-	4+	6+	2	2
Ranged: -		Melee: 2D8		Evil		
Equipment: -						

WRAITH			20mm		20pts	
Power Dice: -			Undead		Support	
Sp	Me	Ra	Ar	Ne	Wn	Ht
7	5+	-	3+	6+	2	2
Crushing Strength (1), Fly						
Ranged: -		Melee: 2D8			Evil	
Equipment: -						

WEREWOLF			40mm		33pts	
Power Dice: -			Undead		Large	
Sp	Me	Ra	Ar	Ne	Wn	Ht
7	4+	-	4+	4+	4	3
Bloodlust, Crushing Strength (2), Vicious						
Ranged: -		Melee: 4D8			Evil	
Equipment: -						

NECROMANCER			20mm		39pts	
Power Dice: ⬡ ⬡			Undead	Command, Spellcaster		
Sp	Me	Ra	Ar	Ne	Wn	Ht
5	6+	5+	5+	5+	3	2
Ranged: 1D8		Melee: 1D8			Evil	

Spells: Heal (short), Lightning Bolt (long), Raise Dead (long), Shield (short)

Raise Dead (long) - Place a new Skeleton model (not an Archer) anywhere within 3" of the Necromancer (and more than 1" from any enemy models). Mark the new model as Activated. The newly raised Skeleton is now a member of the warband for the duration of the current game only.

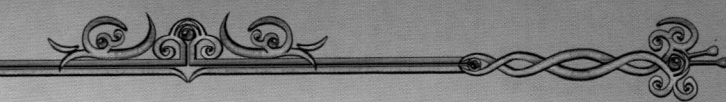

BASIC EQUIPMENT LISTS

The following list details the basic equipment items that are available to players to purchase in one-off games or for those playing in Campaigns (see page 131) and the effect each one has on the model with the item while they have it. In a Campaign, if an instruction is given to randomly select equipment, use the dice result in this table to determine the items found.

When assembling a Warband, equipment has a points value and is paid for just like a model.

Models may be equipped with a maximum of 2 different pieces of extra equipment (in addition to any already listed on their cards)

and they must be of different Types. GRUNTS may only be given a single Common item. BEASTS may not be given any equipment.

Only Common equipment items may be duplicated within a Warband for a game, Rare items may not be. In a Campaign, a Company may only have one of each Unique item. Warbands in one-off games may not purchase Unique items.

Items listed as Single Use are permanently discarded once used.

Common Items

Campaign Price: 2 CG each

D88 Roll	Name	Type	Rules	Points	Notes
11-18	Spear	Melee	Models with spears not Engaged with an enemy model but within 2" of a friendly model that is, grant the Engaged model one bonus die for its Melee attacks. Only 1 bonus die may be given to a model in this way, regardless of the number of spears in range. Models with spears participating in a *Group Charge* Action to do not have to engage enemy models but must end their move within 2" of a model in the group that is Engaged.	2	
21-28	Bandages	Sundries	A model with this item may discard it during its activation to Roll a die. On a 4+, recover 1 Wound the model has previously suffered.	2	Single Use
31-34	Lucky Charm	Magic	Use this item to re-roll any one die for any roll made by this model.	1	Use once per game.
35-38	Bodkin Arrow	Sundries	When this item is used, the model gains *Piercing (1)* or adds +1 to its *Piercing* value when making a Ranged attack with this ammunition (excluding spells).	2	Single Use
41-44	Sheaf of Arrows	Sundries	When this item is used, the model gains a bonus die when making a Ranged attack with this ammunition (excluding spells).	2	Single Use
45-52	Heavy Weapon	Melee	The model gains *Crushing Strength (1)* or adds +1 to its *Crushing Strength* value when making a Melee attack with this weapon.	3	
53-62	Bow/Light-crossbow	Ranged	Range 12"	2	
63-68	Common Mount	Mount	The model gains +2 Sp to a maximum of 8, +1 Height and the *Cavalry* special rule. The mode's base size becomes Cav. Models lose the *Fly* special rule while using a Mount.	5	Cannot be taken by LARGE models or those with the *Cavalry* special rule.
71-74	Crossbow	Ranged	Range 12". *Piercing (1), Reload.*	2	
75-78	Large Shield	Armour	The model has the *Defender* special rule.	3	Cannot be taken by SPELLCASTERS
81-84	Crude Throwing Knife	Ranged	Range 6"	1	
85-88	Wicked dagger	Melee	The model has the *Sneaky* special rule when making a Melee attack with this item.	1	

Rare Items

Campaign Price: 4 CG each

D8 Roll	Name	Type	Rules	Points	Notes
1	Healing Herbs	Sundries	A model with this item may discard it during its activation to recover 1 Wound the model has previously suffered.	3	Single Use
2	Battle Potion	Sundries	A model with this item may discard it when making a Melee attack to gain 2 bonus dice.	3	Single Use
3	Potion of Haste	Sundries	When this item is used, the model may *Run* as a short action and has the *Pathfinder* special rule until the end of the Turn.	2	Single Use
4	Long Bow	Ranged	Range 15"	3	
5	Potion of Concentration	Sundries	A model with this item may discard it to automatically pass a Nerve test.	2	Single Use
6	Blade of Slashing	Melee	When Retaliating, the model has a +1 modifier to its Melee attacks.	4	
7	Rare Mount	Mount	The model gains +2 Sp to a maximum of 8, +1 Height, +1 Wound and the *Cavalry* special rule. The mode's base size becomes Cav. Models lose the *Fly* special rule while using a Mount.	8	Cannot be taken by LARGE models or those with the *Cavalry* special rule.
8	Marksman's Rifle	Ranged	Range 15". *Piercing (1), Marksman, Reload.*	6	

Unique Items

Campaign Price: 8 CG each

D8 Roll	Name	Type	Rules	Points	Notes
1	Healing Potion	Sundries	A model with this item may discard it during its activation to recover up to 3 Wounds the model has previously suffered.	5	Single Use
2	Holy Hand Grenades	Ranged	Range 6", *Piercing (2), Area Effect* [2", 2D8, *Piercing(1)*]	8	
3	Ophidian Book of Secrets	Magic	Add 3" to the range of any spells this model casts that have a printed [Range x"] value.	8	SPELLCASTERS only
4	Firescorch scroll	Ranged	Range 9", *Breath, Piercing (2).*	6	Use once per game.
5	Helm of Command	Magic	A model with this item may use it during its activation. Until the end of the Round, this model and all within 9" of it automatically pass any Nerve tests they are required to make.	8	Use once per game.
6	Wings of Honeymaze	Magic	The model has the *Fly* special rule.	10	Cannot be taken by LARGE models or those with the *Cavalry* special rule.
7	Battle Mount	Mount	The model gains +2 Sp to a maximum of 8, +1 Height, +1 Wound and the *Cavalry* special rule. In addition, the models gains an extra 2D8 for its Melee attacks and has the *Pound* special rule. The mode's base size becomes Cav. Models lose the *Fly* special rule while using a Mount.	15	LARGE models with this item have a 50mm base. Cannot be taken by models with the *Cavalry* special rule.
8	Cloak of the Chameleon	Magic	A model with this item has the *Sneaky, Stealthy* and *Dodge* special rules. In addition, it may re-roll failed Armour rolls when making *Break Away* actions.	10	

In the future, additional or extended equipment lists may be provided as well as equipment reference cards. If cards are being used and equipment is to be randomly selected, all the appropriate cards can be shuffled and dealt as an alternative to rolling on a table.

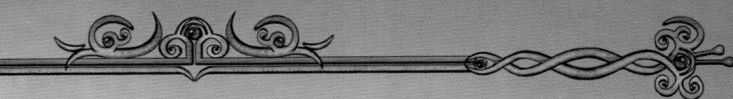

VANGUARD ADVANCED SPELLBOOK

Magic permeates through all things in Mantica and is bound up with each of its races in one fashion or another. The scribes in the great colleges of Basilea and the Elven kingdoms have recorded that magic flows in four major currents or strands they call "Stratum".

The spells categorised as being in the Universal strand have been outlined already in the Basic Spellbook. The other major strands are classified as Noble, Primordial and Corrupt.

In a one-off game, SPELLCASTERS can get access to advanced spells as follows:

- A SPELLCASTER may swap ONE of the spells on its card with ONE of its faction specific spells for free OR

- A SPELLCASTER may purchase an additional spell for 10 points. This can be any one of their faction specific or advanced spellbook spells permitted based on their faction alignment.

During a campaign, SPELLCASTERS will learn new spells from their faction spells or the advanced spellbook as they gain experience.

Spells & Alignment

Factions have an Alignment, and this dictates which strands of magic, and spells they have access to.

SPELLCASTERS are only permitted access to spells based on their faction's Alignment as follows:

- Those of Good Alignment may learn and use Noble spells. In a campaign they may learn ONE Primordial spell.

- Those of Neutral Alignment may learn and use Priordial spells. In a campaign they may learn ONE Nobel or Corrupt spell.

- Those of Evil alignment may learn and use Corrupt spells. In a campaign they may learn ONE Primordial spell.

Noble Spells

When rolling randomly to learn a spell, use the following table:

1-2:	Dazzle
3-4:	Deteriorate
5:	Transpose
6:	Blur
7:	Teleport
8:	Chain Lightning

Dazzle (short): Range 9", 2D8

If any hits are scored, the target is considered blinded. For the remainder of the Round, it cannot make any Ranged attacks and rolls 1 less die when making Melee attacks. The target doesn't suffer any wounds.

Boosted version: Cast as a long action instead. As above, but in addition each attack made against the model counts as being made from the rear arc.

Deteriorate (long): Range 6", 2D8

May be targeted against enemy models that are Engaged. For each 6+ scored, the target's Ar stat is increased by 1 until the end of the Round (e.g. 4+ becomes 5+).

Boosted version: Cost 2 Power. As above, but for each 5+ scored, the target's Ar stat is increased by 1 until the end of the Round.

Transpose (long): Range 6"

No dice roll is required. The caster and one friendly model that is not engaged within 6" of the caster swap places. They may be placed facing any direction but otherwise must be put exactly in the other model's position (or as close as possible, base-size permitting). Both models are marked as Activated.

Boosted version: Cost 2 Power. As above, but the friendly model being swapped is not marked as Activated unless it already is. The caster is still marked as Activated as normal.

Blur (short): Range 9", 1D8

Target a friendly model. If any hits are scored, the model cannot be targeted directly by any other Ranged attacks from any source for the remainder of the Round. The target doesn't suffer any wounds.

Teleport (long): Range 6", 1D8

Target a friendly, un-Engaged model of Height 2 or less and roll a single die. On a score of 4+, pick up and replace the model anywhere within 6" of the casting model facing a direction of your choosing. The target model must now take a Nerve test. If failed, the target model is marked as Fatigued.

Boosted version: Cost 2 Power. As above but the caster may target an enemy model instead. Your opponent may choose the facing of any of their teleported models.

Chain Lightning (long): Range 9", 2D8, Piercing (2)

If any wounds are suffered by the target, choose another un-Engaged enemy model within 3" of the target and roll to attack again. Repeat this process until there are no eligible models. Each model can only be attacked once from a single casting of this spell. Targets beyond the first may be outside LOS of the casting model but must in LOS from the previous target.

Tanglefoot (long): Range 12", 2D8

If any hits are scored, the target is instead ensnared in thick and fast growing brambles. The model must spend a long action on its next activation (or as soon as it can) to free itself. It cannot perform any other action until it does so. While entangled, the model loses 1 die from any Melee or Ranged attack it makes and all attacks against it are considered to be from its rear arc. The target doesn't suffer any wounds.

Veiling Fog (long): Range 12"

Choose a friendly model within 12" of the caster. No dice roll is required. For the remainder of the Round, when shooting at this model, attacking models count their Ra value as 2 higher when rolling for hits (including casting spells).

Nature's Cloak (short)

Cast on self. No dice roll is required. The casting model cannot be the target of any Ranged attacks or be Engaged by any new models for the remainder of the Round.

Brisk Work (short): Range: 9"

Target a friendly model that is not Knocked-down and is un-Engaged. No dice roll is required. That model may immediately take a *Walk* action for free, even if it is already Activated and/or Fatigued.

Stoneskin (long): Range 9"

No dice roll is required. Place a spell effect counter on any friendly model within 9" of the caster. This model may discard the counter at any time in the Round to automatically save one hit against it. The counter is removed at the end of the Round if not used.

Primordial Spells

When rolling randomly to learn a spell, use the following table:

1-2:	Waterlogged
3-4:	Tanglefoot
5:	Veiling Fog
6:	Nature's Cloak
7:	Brisk Work
8:	Stoneskin

Waterlogged (long)

Place a 6" diameter piece of Height 0 Difficult Terrain in base contact with the caster. The terrain piece remains in place until the model casts the same spell again, in which case it is move to a new position.

Boosted version: Costs (n) Power (maximum of 2). For each Power spent, the model may add an additional counter to the one granted in the regular version of the spell. Each counter grants an automatic save to the model to be used when spent as above.

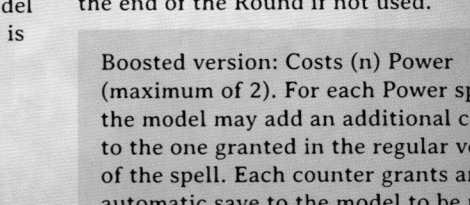

Corrupt Spells

When rolling randomly to learn a spell, use the following table:

1-2:   Lure

3-4:   Shatter

5:    Malevolence

6:    Possesion

7:    Summon Familiar

8:    Nightfall

Lure (long): Range 6"

The player nominates a point on the board within 6" of the casting model and places a counter there no larger than 25mm diameter (a coin is suitable). The marker cannot be placed touching a model or Impassable Terrain.

When an un-Engaged enemy model that is within 6" of the marker and has LoS to it is activated, it must make a Nerve test. If the test is failed, the first action the model must take is a *Walk* action directly towards the counter. The model will move around other models so as not to Engage them. Move the model as far as it can go. If a model must also make a Fallback Check, this is made instead and the test for the Lure is not required.

The marker is removed in the End Phase.

Shatter (long): Range 3", 1D8

If the target model is hit, no wounds are caused. Instead, the target model's Ar stat is increased by 1 (to a maximum of 8+) for the remainder of the game. Multiple castings on the same model will not have a cumulative effect.

Malevolence (long): 1D8

If a hit is scored, all enemy models within 6" of the caster must make an Armour roll to avoid talking a wound.

Possession (long): Range 9", 1D8

Target an un-Activated enemy model. If the target model is hit, no wounds are caused. Mark the model with a counter instead as a reminder. When the model is Activated roll a die. On a 6+, you can choose what the model does for its first short action, including attacking models in its own warband. The marker is then removed and the model may finish its Turn as normal. On a 5 or less, simply remove the marker.

Summon Familiar (short)

Cast on self. No dice roll required. Place a suitable counter or model to represent the familiar next to the casting model (within 1") as a reminder (it has no physical effect on the game). In a subsequent Round, the familiar may be removed (spent) to improve the caster's Ra stat by 2 for the next spell it casts (for example Ra 5+ becomes Ra 3+). A caster may only have one summoned familiar at a time.

Nightfall (short)

No dice roll is required. For the remainder of the Round, while within 3" of the caster, all models gain the *Stealthy* special rule.

> Boosted version: Cast as a long action instead. As above, but the area is increased to 6".

CAMPAIGNS

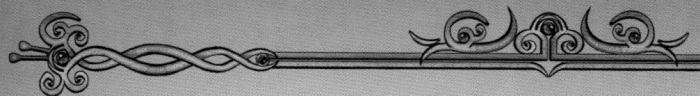

Campaigns allow players to link individual games of Vanguard into a larger narrative that chronicles the adventures of their Warband members' lives and trials. Campaigns can take a bit of work, but a fun and exciting campaign can be very rewarding, and will likely feature in your gaming group's conversations for years to come!

Players who have Kings of War armies, can also combine both games into a bigger, more involved narrative story arc where the adventures of the Warbands skirmishing over strategic ground, ambushing enemy raiding parties or destroying enemy supplies can influence the larger battles – for better or for worse!

Mantica is a dangerous place, but it is also filled with great opportunities. The land may be razed by the passing of great armies, but often critical infrastructure, supplies and valuable items remain intact and left behind. Warbands will have their own missions to perform, whether it is containing a threat, releasing a prisoner, assassinating an enemy general or stealing the enemy's plans. As your Warband becomes more and more successful in achieving their goals, they will encounter many useful abandoned items, artefacts and equipment to retrieve and make use of.

Warriors in a Warband become adept at salvaging what they find and are sometimes boosted by the occasional lucky find of a rare or magical item. While resupply and intelligence from the army's general is possible, it cannot always be relied upon as supply lines are cut and communications are disrupted. Warbands learn to operate on their own, often far ahead or far afield from their army's base camp. Such a life can be gruelling and cruel, but the survivors become grizzled veterans and opponents to be feared.

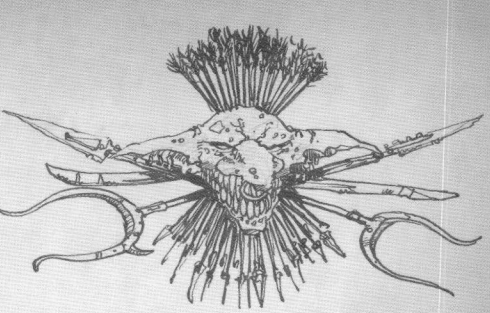

Campaign Terms

As well as using the normal rules, campaigns need to more closely define a few terms and add a couple of extra ones:

Vanguard Company

This is your overall force of models. Think of this as your extended base camp where all the resources you have are collected. You will not have everything available at once, and this more accurately reflects the difficulties in maintaining logistics and supply lines in the midst of a protracted campaign.

However, you will be able to tailor what resources you do have for specific missions – at least to an extent.

Supply Caravan

This is the collection of items and equipment gathered over the course of a campaign. Supplies are bought using Campaign Gold (see below) found on the battlefield, or recovered during the Forage & Explore phase (see page 145). These are the only items that you can choose from to take with you on a mission when you muster a Warband.

Warband

This is the specific group of models and items that undertake each scenario, chosen from your overall Vanguard Company and with equipment from the Supply Caravan. Unlike a standard game, during a campaign you must draw the models and items from your Vanguard Company and Supply Caravan rather than simply building any force you like. This makes campaign forces different to those built for one-off games – they are a crew of individuals selected for their skills for a particular mission and drawn from the wider Vanguard Company.

Campaign Gold

Campaign Gold, or CG, is the currency of Vanguard campaigns. It represents a range of resources such as money collected, secrets found or stolen, and reputation (or infamy) earned among the armies fighting in the wider campaign. They are earned through winning games or exploring between games, and are spent on new equipment, models and other supplies.

On your roster sheet, you will have two spaces for Total CG, and Unspent CG. Total CG is a record of all CG earned throughout the campaign, and only ever increases; this may be used by some campaign organisers to track progress, or simply for bragging rights! Unspent CG rises and falls as CG is earned and spent.

Retinue

This is the name given to the core group of specialists and heroes that form the leadership team of your Vanguard Company and Warband. Having a Retinue really helps develop your Company and the characters within it.

The Retinue represents a variety of roles that can be assigned to your models that will offer them the chance to select unique abilities and receive experience for specific actions as they progress.

More details on choosing your Retinue can be found on page 132.

Company Roster Sheet

The roster is a record of all the models and items that make up your Vanguard Company, specific Warbands and Supplies. Individual models have their stats and special rules listed here along with any current injuries or experience. You will also be able to record Campaign Points or other information relevant to your campaign. Some players even keep a record of models they've lost on their sheet, to remember their valued service, but this is not required.

A blank campaign roster that you can copy for personal use is provided on page 156.

Starting a Campaign

Before beginning your campaign, your group will need to make a few decisions around the kind of campaign they want to play. Campaigns can be as complex or as simple as the players prefer, with some groups making elaborate territory maps for armies and Warbands to fight over, or a branching narrative decision-tree with an over-arching plot that evolves as players win or lose games.

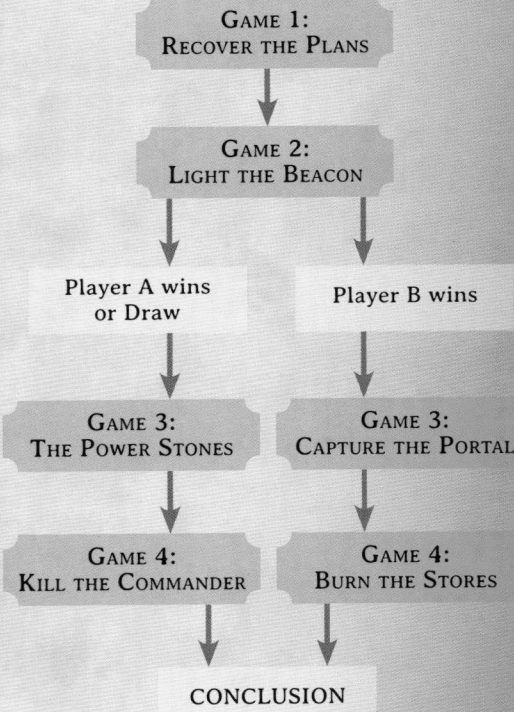

Here's an example of a very simple campaign story tree for 2 players. It has one branching point which determines the following games that are played.

- *The winner of game 1 chooses to be Attacker or Defender in game 2.*

- *The winner of game 2 (or Player A in a draw) is always the Attacker for any following games that require one.*

- *Games 1-3 score the winner 1 Campaign Point.*

- *The winner of game 4 scores 3 Campaign Points.*

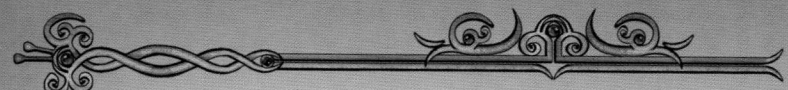

Campaigns can be a series of Vanguard games only, or can be a mix of Vanguard and Kings of War games - with the results of one potentially influencing the other. More information and ideas on having mixed campaigns like this can be found on page 155.

Some players may find themselves motivated to write some short fiction or photograph battle reports based on their exploits, and share them in an online forum or wiki – while others are content to simply swap stories over post-game drinks of the heroic exploits and humiliating misfortunes experienced on the table-top.

For your first few attempts at campaign play, it's recommended to keep things simple. Playing a campaign through to completion not only feels great, but acts as a great recruitment tool when seeking more players for the next one; and of course there is no reason why, at the end of the campaign, a group of players can't decide to extend the campaign for just a few games more.

Organisation

One player in the campaign should act as the campaign organiser. This person will be responsible for reminding players to schedule games, keep their Warband rosters updated, keep track of wins and losses, and act as a mediator and arbitrator for rules disputes. This may sound like a lot of work, and it can be, but it can ultimately be a rewarding experience.

The players should also agree on how long they want the campaign to go on for. Short campaigns with fixed end points are a good way to build experience in running them.

A simple first campaign

For your first campaign we recommend that players play 4-8 games each and tries to play everyone else at least once.

Once everyone has played the agreed upon number of games, tally up each player's wins and losses as follows:

Win – 3 Campaign Points

Lose/Draw – 1 Campaign Point

This winner of the campaign will be the player with the most Campaign Points at the end.

Alternatively, the campaign organiser might choose another metric for success, such as tracking the total amount of CG earnt across the entire campaign, or having the top two placeholders fight a final, no-holds-barred, winner takes- all game in a climactic fight to the death.

Future Vanguard or Kings of War supplements may include more complicated or involved campaign outlines with special objectives or Warband-specific goals to represent the many and varied environments found throughout Mantica.

Building your Company

Once you have a group of players excited for the upcoming campaign, you will need some Companies and Warbands to play with.

Each player begins with these basic steps:

1. Choose a Faction and Leader
2. Begin a Company Roster Sheet
3. Enlist a Vanguard Company
4. Play some games!

Choose a Faction and Leader

Players may have a collection of models and a favourite faction. For example, Isabelle might be a fanatical goblin player while Rob is a stalwart dwarf player. It's more fun if there is a mixture of different factions in your group, but the amount of infighting within every faction on Mantica makes it perfectly reasonable to have multiple warbands from the same faction.

Finding a faction that appeals to you aesthetically and thematically is more important than trying to decide which faction is the most powerful in the game – you might be spending a lot of time painting and customising your models, and having models that appeal to you will go a long way to motivating you to keep playing and painting!

Either step can be performed first: you may want to build a Warband around a particular favourite model or choose a faction first and then assign a Leader from the range of possible models within it.

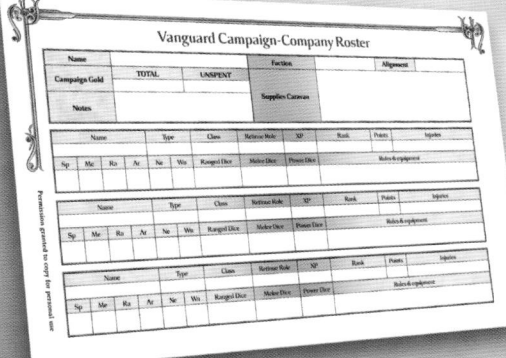

Factions

Each player chooses one faction for their Company.

Your Leader and the other models you select in your Company, must come from the faction you choose.

For example, if you choose Goblins as your faction, you would have a goblin faction leader and all the other models in the Company would be goblins or other entries from the goblin faction list.

Leader

The Leader of your Vanguard Company is a unique individual and can be selected from any COMMAND model Class in a faction list. Perhaps they were born into a privileged status and money has paved their path to leadership? Or maybe they started off in the gutter but have risen to a position of respect and inspiration amongst their troops through sheer graft, skill and bravery?

Your chosen model is assigned the role of Leader and is the start of your Retinue group. When playing in a Campaign the Leader role is the only required Retinue role that all players must select. Whether any further members are added to the Retinue is up to you (see page 132 for more details on assigning a Retinue).

The model that is assigned as the Leader brings additional benefits:

1. Assigning a Leader grants +1 Red Power die to your Power Dice pool while the Leader model is in play in a game.
2. The Leader model gains bonus XP for a number of WARRIOR and GRUNT models that survive each mission.
3. The Leader model may gain bonus XP for completing mission objectives.

Begin a Company roster sheet

Each player will need a Company roster sheet (you can copy the one on page 156 or download a .PDF version from the Mantic Games website). This is where you will record all the details of your Company, Warbands and your Supplies. Every time a model is Killed or Injured, and each time they gain experience, you note this on the roster sheet. It is the central record of everything that makes your Company unique. Keep it safe!

Enlist a Vanguard Company

A Company is made up of soldiers and equipment purchased from the player's starting funds. In a normal, one-off game of Vanguard, each player has 200 points to spend on their models. In a campaign however, each player has 400 points to spend building their Company. Then, for each game to be played, the player will assemble their smaller Warband from models in their Company. Because of this, having a balanced mix of models in a Company is essential to success in a Vanguard campaign, because a player will only be able to use the soldiers already listed on their roster, rather than any models available to the faction as would be normal for one-off games.

Vanguard Companies and Warbands are built just like in one-off games, with the same requirements for the proportion of COMMAND, WARRIORS, SUPPORT, SPELLCASTERS and LARGE model Classes. See page 45 for details. The exception is that you may include any number of COMMAND models in your Company.

Composition Rules:

1. Every Company must have at least 1 COMMAND model and 5 WARRIOR and/or GRUNT models

2. For every 3 WARRIORS and/or GRUNTS in a Company, 1 each of the SUPPORT and SPELLCASTER Classes may be enlisted.

3. For every full 150 points of models enlisted in a Company, 1 LARGE model Class can also be enlisted. However, the first COMMAND model that is also LARGE in the Company does not count against this limit.

4. One model must be assigned as the Company Leader.

If a model has more than one Class, it counts as 1 of each Class for the purposes of Company composition.

Preparing Equipment

You may only ever have one of each item with the Unique rarity. You may purchase one of each Rare item when making your initial Company, but are not restricted as to how many you may own at any given time as the campaign develops. Likewise, you may purchase up to six Common items initially, but may own any amount of them at any point as you find and purchase more for your Supplies using CG earned.

Items purchased when enlisting your Vanguard Company are bought using their points value. During a campaign, subsequent purchases of equipment cost the following CG:

- **Common Items: 2 CG each**
- **Rare Items: 4 CG each**
- **Unique Items: 8 CG each**

Note that each item still has its own points value which is used when building a warband for a game. For example, you may buy a Long Bow for 4 CG (Rare) to add to your Company Supplies. To then give it to a model in a game would cost you 3 points from your Warband's total points limit.

Equipment listed as standard on a model's card doesn't count towards any limits but also cannot be transferred to any other model.

You will not necessarily need to own a physical model for every model you purchase for your Company – If you only own two Nightstalker Reaper models, for example, you should feel free to purchase three, four, or more for your initial Company and only field two in your actual Warband for any given game. The others will act as 'spares' or reinforcements should the first two become unavailable or are killed (or banished to the ether!).

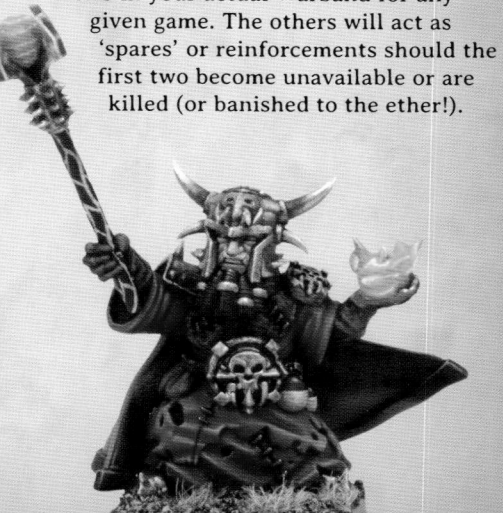

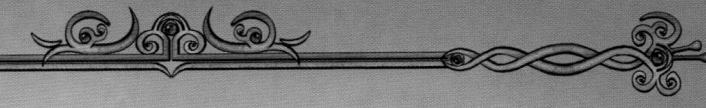

Begin a Retinue

A Company's inner circle of senior warriors is known as the Retinue. Beyond assigning your Leader of a Vanguard Company who already forms part of the Retinue, there are other roles that can be assigned to your most trusted, most liked or most feared soldiers.

Some roles are only available to particular model Classes and others are open to any model. They represent models with specialist skillsets or the most experienced at what they do and as such your Company can't typically have more than one of each Retinue role at any one time unless an exception is stated otherwise.

No model may ever hold more than one Retinue role at any one time. If a model with a Retinue role is assigned to a different role they must leave the previously held role vacant, ready for another model to be promoted to it if desired.

Assigning a model to the Retinue is very simple. Firstly review the benefits that each role provides and the model Class restrictions. Secondly, choose the model from your Company that you want to fill that role, checking the model Class criteria and recording their new position of authority against their entry in the Retinue Role column on the Company Roster Sheet.

The Leader Role is always free to assign. The first additional role in the Retinue is also free when your Company is first formed. After this, you must pay CG to promote models into new roles. This means your Retinue will grow and develop over time as your Company earns its reputation. Whether they will remain a valuable member of your command group is yet to be seen, but should they fail to impress further options in regards Retinue Promotions and Demotions during a campaign are described on page 140.

The full set of roles available within a Retinue are defined in detail on page 151.

Experience & Ranks

As games are played, individual models within your Company earn Experience (XP) for completing deeds within each scenario played. Accumulating experience allows a model to increase in Rank. Ranks are an incremental scale that represents the skill and talent a model gains as they become a more proficient soldier and seasoned veteran.

Ranks are usually accompanied by improvements to the model's base stats, or the gaining of new rules and skills which are added to their repertoire. Additionally, because a Rank 1 model will be less effective on the battlefield than a Rank 5 model, relative ranks are used to balance Vanguard Warbands with different levels of experience against each other. More about this will be explained in the Pre-Game Sequence (see page 136), and Resolve Experience (see page 141) sections later.

The stink of blood and fire filled the air. The demons were closing in, threatening to overwhelm the precious few defenders. Sanya rammed her trident into the crimson chest of one of the cackling abyssals, wrenching it free as the monster gurgled its last breath. But another horned demon took its place all too quickly. She was exhausted.

They were losing; she knew this. There was no way they could hold. She had led her Naiad brothers and sisters in pursuit of a small warband of Abyssals; a remnant cut off from the war with the Abyss. It was her duty as Centurion to see them destroyed before they could pose a threat to the Trident Realm. But with each passing moment, more of her Naiads were falling to the infernal beings.

In addition to individual models increasing in rank, the player earns Campaign Gold (CG) for their Company. These points can be spent on adding new models to the overall Company roster or adding new equipment to the Supplies Caravan, increasing the options available to players in future games. This will be covered in more detail in the Recruitment/Resupply Phase (See page 149) section later.

There are some restrictions for earning experience however. Models of Class GRUNT never gain experience. Models of Class WARRIOR can gain a maximum of 3 Ranks. All other models can gain a maximum of 6 Ranks.

Getting Personal

Finally, consider naming the models in your Company. With any luck, they will fight with honour and enjoy a long, adventure-filled service throughout the campaign of which their names will surely be sung in camp fire songs; and if not, you'll want to know what name to scrawl on the broken piece of rotting timber that will serve as their burial marker for the shallow grave you'll be leaving them in...

Play some games!

Once you have successfully enlisted your Vanguard Company you are ready to play some games of Kings of War Vanguard!

Fighting individual battles in a campaign setting is much the same as any standard one-off game.

However, there are a few distinct sequences that describe pre-, during and post- game options and steps that are outlined in the Pre-Engagement, Engage! and Post-Engagement sequences as follows.

Ahead, through the press of bodies, she spotted something. A woman, wielding a whip and sword, with her red flesh exposed to the danger of the battle. She would have been beautiful, if not for the twisting horns atop her head and the dark malice in her eyes. The female demon was held aloft by a pair of clawed wings, as she looked down in contempt at those beneath her.

Sanya knew what she was looking at – an Abyssal Temptress – the warband's leader. If she could end this creature, then maybe it would crush the morale of the Abyssals. It was a slim chance, but it was better than waiting to die on the claws of the lower demons.

Ducking, winding and lashing out with her trident, she forced her way through the lower Abyssals to stalk her prey. Some resisted and met a swift end, others saw her skill and wisely

decided to survive a little longer. As Sanya neared the Temptress, the demon caught her eye and a wicked smile crept across her lips.

Suddenly, a large, muscled Abyssal stepped to block the Centurion's path. Sanya brought up her left hand and cast her net over the Abyssal Guard's horned helmet. A hard pull brought it down on one knee. Placing a foot on its back, she wrapped the net around her arm once, then wrenched the net up. There was a sickening wet crack as the Abyssal Guard went limp.

Throwing the net aside, Sanya wielded her trident two-handed, coming to face to face with the Temptress. The whip lashed out, wrapping around the haft of the trident. The Temptress dived towards her and looked deep into her eyes.

Do you want to play, my sweet?

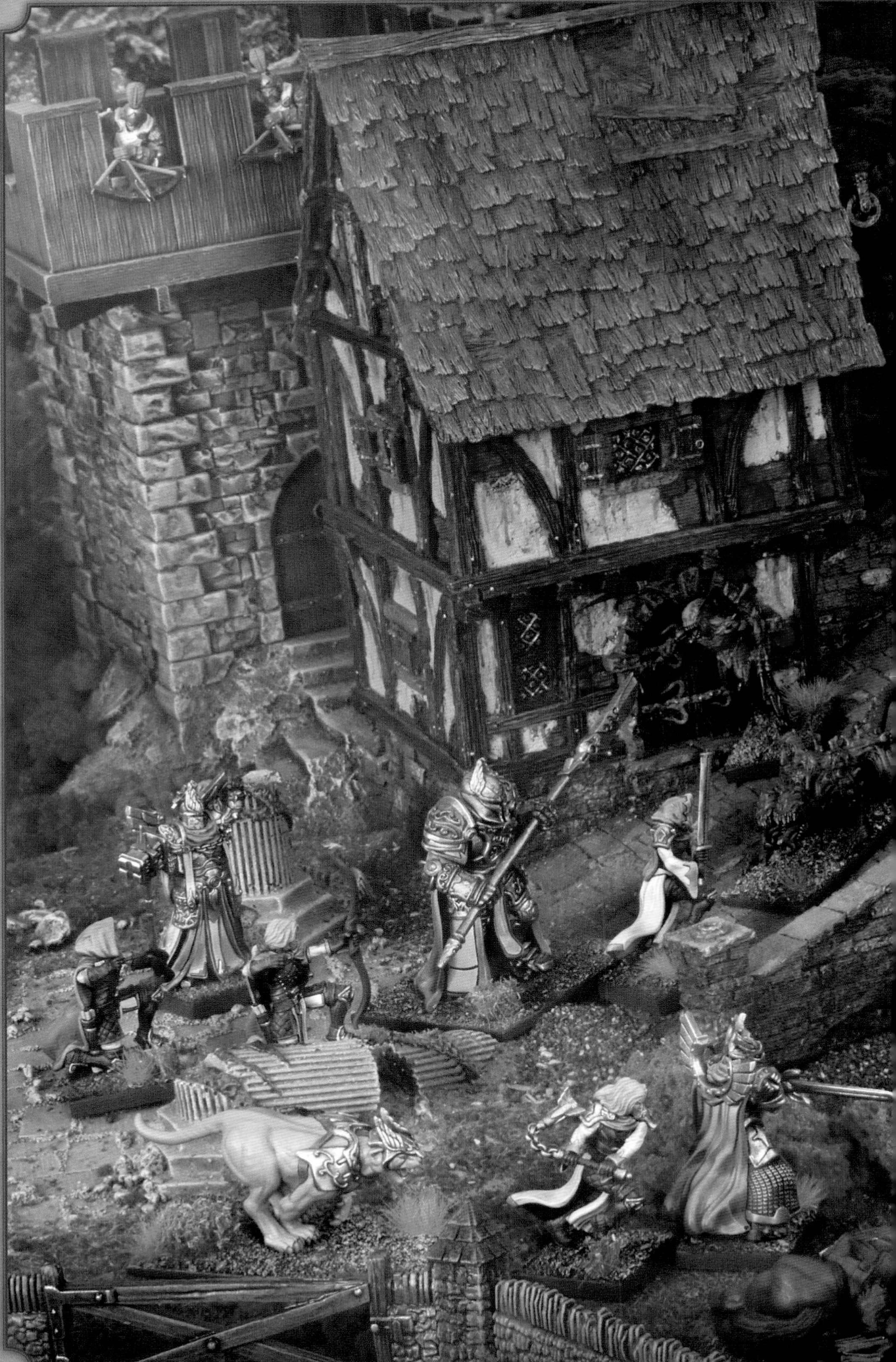

 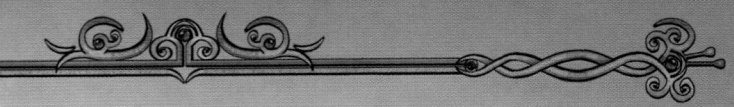

Pre-Engagement

Determine Scenario

Sometimes, as part of a pre-determined narrative, the scenario to be played will have already been decided by the campaign organiser. If not, roll on the scenario table on page 47 to see which scenario will be used for the game.

Muster a Warband

To play a campaign game, each player now musters their soldiers for battle, choosing their Vanguard Warband to the agreed upon points value as normal, with the exception that all models forming the Vanguard Warband must be chosen from those available on the player's Company Roster Sheet. Usually games will be played at 200 points, but your campaign organiser, or the scenario being played, may set a different points value for games. Slowly escalating the points values of games as the campaign progresses can be a good way to represent an intensifying conflict.

The Balance of War

Next, the players add up and compare their Vanguard Warband's Ranks. This is simply the sum of all the Ranks the models in each Warband have reached between them (the Rank Total).

The difference in the totals of the two opposing Warbands determines the number of "Underdog Power Dice" that are awarded to the player with the lower Rank total. Divide the difference in Rank totals by two and round down the result. The player with the lower Rank total receives this many RED Underdog Power Dice.

These dice form an extra pool the player has available for the game and may be added to any Roll for Power made at the start of a Round. A player must decide before rolling whether or not they will add any Underdog Dice from the pool to their roll and they may add a maximum of three to any given roll. Once used, these dice are discarded.

To keep track of Underdog Power Dice available, you may wish to note this on a piece of spare paper, keep a tally of unspent dice using a spare dice, or keep a separate pool of especially lucky dice to use in a pinch; so long as both players know how many dice have been used and how many remain in the less experienced Crew's pool the exact method used to track Underdog Dice is unimportant.

A helping hand

In addition, the difference in the totals of the two opposing Warbands grants that many "bonus" points to the player with the lower Rank total. These bonus points are spent separately to the normal points allowed on the Warband and must be on a single model from their faction list and up to the value of the bonus points. The model must be of type GRUNT, WARRIOR or SUPPORT and does not count towards normal selection rules. The model is only available for the one game and is not added to the roster.

For example, going into a normal game of 200 points per side, Simon's warband has a Rank total 16 lower than Jill's. Simon creates his 200 point Warband as normal and then can spend up to 16 points on a bonus model to use in the game.

Mercenaries

The world of Mantica has many mighty heroes and characters of lore, some of whom are willing to fight for a worthy cause or the promise of coin. Some of these heroes are valued skirmish warriors that a Vanguard Company can hire as mercenaries

If either player wishes to, they may add a single MERCENARY model to their Warband. (this is marked on the mode's card). These sell-swords use up points as normal from the player's point allotment for choosing their Warband for the game. In addition, in order to hire the mercenary, the player must pay for their services out of their Warband's unspent CG as a hiring fee.

The hiring fee for a mercenary depends on their points cost – the more experienced and deadly a mercenary, the more money they can command for their services. A Mercenary costs 1 CG for every 5 points they are (or part thereof). So if a Mercenary is 17 points, it will cost 4 CG to hire for the game.

Mercenaries will have types such as LARGE or SPELLCASTER, and sometimes COMMAND. The Mercenary's type(s) count towards limitations of selection as normal.

Mercenaries are not added to your Warband roster, and must be hired (or re-hired) before each game they participate in. They do not gain XP. Opposing players may hire the same mercenary model - in reality, one or the other will be an individual of comparable skill and ability, trading on the reputation of the real thing. The same reasoning applies to mean that Mercenaries cannot be killed and made unavailable in later games, unless a campaign organiser decides otherwise!

Engage!

The meat of the game is the battle itself that the core rules should have you well prepared for. However, there is one in-game option that some Warbands may wish to take if the cause seems lost: Retreat & Regroup!

Retreat & Regroup!

From time to time during a game, it may become obvious that you are fighting a losing battle. In a campaign, it can be advantageous to cut your losses and run!

At any point at the start of a player's Turn, if 25% of their Warband's models (rounding up) have been removed as casualties, the player may opt to concede victory (forfeit) to their opponent. In doing so, they will still earn CG for participating in a game (despite losing), but may not earn CG for completing any scenario objectives. Carry out the post-engagement sequence as normal.

Post-Engagement

At the end of each game a number of things may happen: models may die or gain experience, items and CG are earned and added to the Company's Supplies for future use, or new recruits and equipment may be purchased. In order to make the steps easier, this process is streamlined into a simple sequence followed by each player at the end of a game:

1. Return Equipment to the Supplies Caravan
2. Resolve Casualties
3. Retinue Assessment
4. Resolve Experience
5. Calculate Campaign Gold
6. Forage & Explore Phase
7. Recruitment and Resupply Phase
8. Check roster is fully updated

The following section describes each of these phases in more detail.

1. Return Equipment to the Supplies Caravan

If any of your models are carrying items at the end of the game, add them back to your Company Supplies. This includes those you took into battle and never used, items found during the battle, and equipment issued to your models at the start of the battle. Single-Use items that were used during the battle are not returned to the Supplies.

Equipment marked as 'Use Once Per Game' is assumed to be recharged or reloaded between battles, and is not removed from your roster or discarded if it was used during a game.

2. Resolve Casualties

Any model of Class GRUNT that is removed from play as a casualty is considered killed outright and removed from the roster. Any other model Class that was removed from play as a casualty during the course of the game may not, in fact, have perished. During the confusion of a skirmish it's hard to tell exactly what injuries a model may have sustained. It's only afterwards, when the dust has cleared and comrades have been dragged away on a makeshift stretcher, are you able to tell the true extent of a model's injuries.

Models that end the game Injured (with one or more wound markers on them) but not "killed", or that left the battlefield due to other reasons such as a Fallback action, are presumed to receive medical aid from their surviving comrades, and will be ready to fight for the next game fully recovered. Models removed from play as a casualty ("killed"), however, may require more extensive medical treatment, and in the midst of a campaign a Warband may be operating miles behind enemy lines, left to fend for themselves.

For each model removed from the game as "killed", roll a D88 on the Casualty Table opposite and apply the result.

If your Warband contained one of more surviving models with the Healer Retinue role at the end of the game, you may re-roll any one result on the Casualty Table for each one. No dice can be re-rolled more than once. If a model already has a Permanent Injury that was rolled on the Casualty Table, and the same type of Permanent Injury is rolled for a second time, ignore the effects of that second result and roll again unless the entry specifies multiple results are possible. Each Permanent Injury a model suffers also subtracts 1 from its Rank.

Record any Injuries and their effects on your Roster sheet for each model affected.

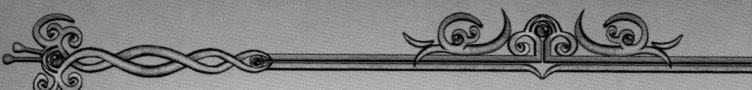

D88 result	Casualty Table
11-16	**Dead** - The model is actually Dead. You bury them in a hastily made and unmarked grave. Remove them and any equipment they from your roster.
17-22	**Haunting Nightmares** - The wounds of combat run deeper than just physical. The model suffers +1 to their Nerve stat. This is a Permanent Injury and may be gained multiple times up to a maximum Nerve value of 8+
23-26	**Mangled Leg** - The model's Speed stat is reduced by 1 (e.g. 5 becomes 4). If the model rides a mount their Speed is still reduced due to the difficulty in riding. This is a Permanent Injury and may be gained a maximum of twice.
27-32	**Lost an Eye** - The models Shoot stat is raised by 1 (e.g. 4+ becomes 5+). This is a Permanent Injury. If the same result is rolled again the model must be retired from the company – remove it from the roster.
33-36	**Severed Sword Arm** - The models Melee stat is raised by 1 (e.g. 4+ becomes 5+). This is a Permanent Injury. In addition the model may no longer use a Ranged weapon. If the same result is rolled again the model must be retired from the company – remove it from the roster.
37-38	**Suppurating Wound** - The model's wounds just will not heal making it uncomfortable to wear armour. The model's armour stat is raised by 1 (e.g. 4+ becomes 5+). This is a Permanent Injury and may be gained a maximum of twice.
41-44	**Old Wounds** - At the start of each game after your warband has been chosen but before scenario deployment, roll a D8 for this model. On a roll of 1 their old wounds have prevented them taking part in the mission, the model is not replaced and you must play that game without it.
45-52	**Broken Bones** - The model suffers -1 to their Wound stat to a minimum of 1. Roll a D8, adding +1 for each Healer you have in your Company. On a result of 5 or more, this only applies to the next game the model plays in. On a result of 4 or less, this is a Permanent Injury.
53-56	**Slow Recovery** - The model survives, but will take time to fully recover. They must miss your next game and will be unavailable for selection.
57-60	**Concussion** - The model will lose a random special rule they have (not granted through equipment) for the next game they play in.
61-62	**Horrible Scars** - The model's scars are so hideous that enemies are reluctant to attack them. Enemies wishing to Engage the model with a qualifying *Charge* action must pass a Nerve test to do so. They may still engage normally otherwise. This effect is permanent.
63-64	**Impressive scars** - The model gains some truly extraordinary scars and the legendary exploits to go with them. The scars are so impressive that the model gains the Inspiring ability. If they already have the Inspiring ability, this has no further effect. This effect is permanent.
65-66	**Captured** - The model makes a full recovery but has been captured by the enemy. You may ransom them back for 3CG + 5 CG per Rank the model has. Transfer the money to your opponent in exchange for your model. If you don't have the money or don't wish to pay it, roll a D8: 1-4, the model is Dead, remove it from your roster as described above; 5-6 the model escapes but has Haunting Nightmares as described above; 7-8 the model escapes with a Survives against the Odds result as below. Alternatively you could build a rescue attempt into your campaign narrative as a Vanguard or Dungeon Saga scenario!
67-68	**Survives against the Odds** - Left for dead on the battlefield, the model somehow makes it back to camp alone through enemy lines and the wilderness. The model must miss your next game but otherwise makes a full recovery. In addition, they gain 2XP from the experiences they have been through.
71-88	**Full recovery** - The model survives with no lasting complications. They may participate in the next game as normal.

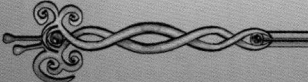

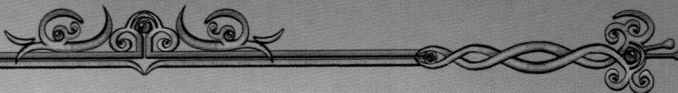

3. Retinue Assessment

Rewarding Success & Punishing Failure

As a Vanguard Company expands and advances through the trials of multiple missions, some characters from the Retinue may die or underperform in their assigned role, whilst some of the lesser troops may show themselves to be excellent survivors or combatants and deserve greater recognition. In this phase, each Company may perform one Promotion and one Demotion.

Promotion

- Where a Retinue slot becomes available (via permanent model death or demotion - more on that later), a Leader can promote one of their existing troops into the vacant role at a cost of 3 CG, following normal model restrictions and Warband composition rules.

- The selected model is then simply promoted into the Retinue command group by marking their new role on the Warband Roster under the Retinue Role column for future reference. They will now have different advancement options available to them.

- If moving an existing Retinue role character to fill another role in the Retinue that has become vacant, this also counts as a Promotion *(the exception being when filling a vacant leader role, see page 149)*.

- If a promoted character was already at Rank 1 or more, their promotion carries on from that point and they carry over any current XP earned so far.

Demotion

- Aside from death taking a beloved model from your warband, you may decide that one or more of the Retinue are underperforming and not pulling their weight. Better soldiers and adventurers are always waiting in the wings and could prove more accomplished given the chance.

- In this instance an active member of the Retinue can be demoted back to "normal" troop duties to free up a Retinue slot for a Promotion to take place.

- However this comes at a cost:

    1. 1 CG must be spent on a Demotion (this reflects the administration needed to strip access to upgrades and equipment from the former officer)

    2. Both the Leader and demoted models lose 1 XP for each Rank the demoted model has (the models will not actually lose any acquired Rank however). This reflects having to back track on a previous decision which can look bad in front of the rest of the Company and can cause some dissent and discord.

Transferring the Leader role

It is possible to transfer the Leader role. This must be to another COMMAND model currently in the Company of the same faction as the current Leader. That model's current Retinue role, if it has one, becomes vacant and replaced with the Leader role. This is done at a cost of 5 CG and no other Promotion or Demotion can occur this phase for the Company.

4. Resolve Experience

Each model in a Company starts a campaign at Rank 0 and can increase in Rank up to 6. Individual models gain experience points (XP) according to the table below. Each model can only gain 1 XP in each category per game (and only if the model was part of the Warband that played the game). Adjust each model's entry on the roster sheet accordingly.

- GRUNTS cannot gain XP and never progress beyond Rank 0

- WARRIORS may gain XP but cannot advance beyond Rank 3

Earning XP

Core experience is gained through completing Vanguard Deeds during an engagement:

- Model participates in, and survives (not removed as a casualty) a game: +1 XP

- Model kills one or more enemy models in a game: +1XP

- Model plays in, and survives (not removed as a casualty) a game against a warband of higher Rank: +1XP

- In addition, if the Leader model participates in, and survives (not removed as a casualty) a game, 1XP can be given to any other surviving member of the warband to represent a battlefield commendation.

Additionally however, unique experience gains can be made by completing special Retinue Role Deeds

- This applies specifically to characters in the Retinue and are defined by role in addition to any normal XP that is gained by that model (as above). See page 151.

To help keep track of experience, the Company roster includes locations to record the XP and Rank for each model.

Some scenarios may also grant additional XP under certain conditions.

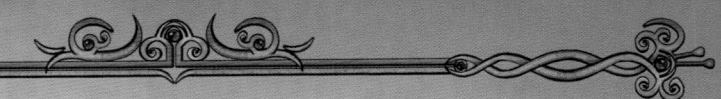

Advancing in Rank

When a model has earned enough XP they will increase in Rank. Each increase in Rank requires more XP to achieve than the previous one as shown below. Thus it only costs 3 XP to move to Rank 1 but a model must earn another 5XP before it can advance to Rank 2.

The amount of XP required to move between Ranks is as follows:

Rank progression	XP Cost
0-1	3 XP
1-2	5 XP
2-3	7 XP
3-4	9 XP
4-5	11 XP
5-6	13 XP

A model may only advance one Rank at a time. If they earn sufficient XP to advance a second Rank, the model will only be able to actually advance to the second Rank after the next game played, whether that model participates in the game or not – make a note on the roster so you don't forget.

The maximum Rank a model may achieve is 6.

When a model reaches a new Rank, it may choose one of the following options:

- Core Stat Upgrade
- New Special Rule
- Power upgrade (COMMAND models only)
- Learn new spell (SPELLCASTER models only)
- Role specific advancement (see Retinue Roles on page 151)

Core Stat Upgrade

A model may choose one of the following stat upgrades. A stat upgrade cannot be taken on a stat that has a value of -. Stats are improved by reducing the value in them (making them easier to achieve in a dice roll). E.g. a value of 5+ become 4+. However, wounds are obviously increased!

- Ranged boost – reduce the value of the model's Ra stat by 1.
- Melee boost – reduce the value of the model's Me stat by 1.
- Nerve boost – reduce the value of the model's Ne stat by 1.
- Wound boost – increase the value of the model's Wn stat by 1.

Only one upgrade per stat may be ever be taken unless specifically stated otherwise (e.g. a model can only ever receive 1 Melee boost).

If a model subsequently suffers a penalty to an upgraded stat (such as from a Permanent Injury), the stat may not be upgraded again.

No stat value can ever improve beyond 3+ or be worse than 8+.

New Special Rule

Your troops are constantly learning from and adapting to conditions in the field. Even the chilling Nightstalkers and undead hordes can mutate or grow in power and influence, in the right conditions.

Such skills and evolution is represented by gaining new special rules.

A model may gain a maximum of 3 new special rules in this way through campaign experience.

Each model Class has a set of ability tables for their models to roll on, based on their Class. Any model can roll on the Standard WARRIOR table however if desired. Models with more than one Class can choose which associated table to roll on.

When a new special rule is selected as the upgrade for the new Rank, roll on the chosen table and add that new rule to the model's entry in the Warband roster. If a rule is rolled the model already has (not granted by additional equipment) then roll again.

If a model already has all the possible rules in the tables it has access to, a different Rank advancement option must be chosen.

Class Advancement Tables

COMMAND

D8 Roll	Ability
1-2	6th Sense
3-4	Unbreakable
5-6	Inspiring*
7-8	Steady

*If a model already possesses *Inspiring*, It gains *Very Inspiring* instead.

LARGE

D8 Roll	Ability
1-2	Unbreakable
3-4	Defender
5-6	Smash*
7-8	Steady

*If a model already possesses *Smash*, it replaces it with *Pound*.

SPELLCASTER

D8 Roll	Ability
1-2	6th Sense
3-4	Dodge
5-6	Regenerate (7+)*
7-8	Stubborn

*This represents the spellcaster learning a basic personal mystical healing ritual.

SUPPORT

D8 Roll	Ability
1-2	Parry
3-4	Dodge
5-6	Pathfinder
7-8	Stealthy

WARRIOR

D8 Roll	Ability
1	Crushing Strength (1)*
2	Defender
3	Headstrong
4	Marksman
5	Parry
6	Steady
7	Smash
8	Vicious

*If a model already possesses *Crushing Strength (n)*, add 1 to the n value on its profile.

Power Upgrade

COMMAND models can purchase a single additional red Power Die that will remain part of their Power Dice Pool for future battles (as long as the same COMMAND model remains alive and part of the Warband). Models may only take this purchase option **once**, no matter what Rank they are.

However, COMMAND models can upgrade any single Power Die they already have (including an additional Power Die they had purchased previously as above) to its next subsequent level (red > white, white > blue). This upgrade option can be taken as part of any Rank increase – it is not limited to only being taken once.

Only one Power Die may be purchased or upgraded per Rank Increase.

OR

OR

ONCE ONLY

Learn new spell

SPELLCASTERS have the option to learn a new spell when they gain a Rank. They may choose to learn any spell they don't already know from the Vanguard basic spell book or one of their faction specific spells. Alternatively, they may choose learn a spell from the advanced spell book (see page 122). They may only learn from spells of an alignment that matches that of their faction (Good, Neutral or Evil). A model learning a spell from the advanced spell book has two options:

- Roll randomly to see which spell is learned. If the spell is already one the model knows, roll again.

- Spend an additional 2XP and choose which spell to learn.

Record any new spell the model now has access to in their entry on the Company roster.

There is no limit to the number of spells a SPELLCASTER can have.

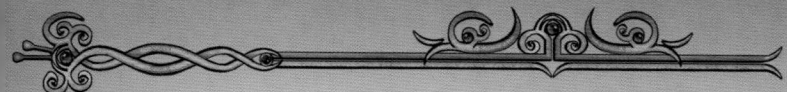
5. Calculate Campaign Gold (CG)

After each game players will gain resources to spend on purchasing new models and equipment.

The number of CG earned depends on the each player's result in the scenario that was played.

Player Result	CG Earned
Win	16 CG
Draw	12 CG
Loss	10 CG

Add the CG earned to both the total CG and unspent CG areas of the Company roster sheet.

Remember that the total CG only ever goes up, whilst the unspent CG rises and falls as it is earnt and spent.

CG earnt can be spent in the Recruitment and Resupply phase of the post-engagement sequence, or saved for future games.

6. Forage & Explore Phase

After the battle, your Warband has the opportunity to explore their surroundings, searching for any resources, items, enemy secrets and other supplies they can find. Roll on this table even if you forfeited the game or were wiped out.

Step 1 – Forage and Loot

Roll a D8. The result is the number of CG you gain while exploring. Add this to your roster.

- If you had any models with *Pathfinder* in the Warband you may re-roll the D8. Models must have had the rule already during the game (not only just earnt it through experience).

Step 2 - Exploration

Roll a second D8 and add it to the first to create a D88 result (e.g. you rolled a 5 on the Forage and Loot roll and then a 6 on the Exploration to give a result of 56). Now reference the Exploration Table on the following page, applying the results described next to the number you have rolled. The following table is the standard one for Vanguard, but future Vanguard expansions may have different environments to explore. Watch your step!

- If you had any models with *Scout* in the Warband you may reroll the second D8. Models must have had the rule already during the game (not only just earnt it through experience).

> For the re-rolls above to apply, the models that provide the re-roll ability must have participated in and survived (not been "killed") the previous game without suffering a Permanent Injury. This also applies when resolving results on the Exploration Table.

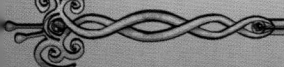  

D88 result	Exploration Result
11-12	**Abandoned Outpost** - Picking through the wreckage of an abandoned outpost you find equipment (randomly select 2 Common equipment items).
13-14	**Minor shrine** - The small trinkets and dedications left by the faithful can be traded for more valuable supplies. Gain 1D8 CG
15-16	**Alchemists Laboratory** - The complex alchemical instruments are lost on you but may be of value. Gain 1D8 CG. If your Retinue contains a Healer, also gain one Healing Herbs equipment item
17-18	**Travelling Fletcher** - You manage to convince the scared craftsman to provide you with new arrows. Gain 2 Sheaves of Arrows and 1 Bodkin Arrow.
21-22	**Major Shrine** - You lead your troops in prayer to your chosen God of War. Roll a die. On a 5+ you are blessed for your efforts. In your next game of Vanguard, up to 3 models in your Warband may be given the *Pathfinder* and *Stealthy* special rules until the end of the game. On any other result, your prayers go unanswered. If your model with the Leader role was used in and survived the last game, you may add +1 to the die roll.
23-24	**Sword in the Stone** - You follow local tales of a famous magical sword thrust into solid rock. On closer inspection, the peasants were exaggerating - it's not a legendary masterwork, but it is an incredibly well made minor magic item. Gain a Blade of Slashing.
25-26	**Abandoned Mine** - Roll a die for the type of mine found. 1-2: Slate mine; nothing of value 3-4: Coal mine; gain 1D8 CG 5-6: Silver mine; gain 1D8+2 CG 7-8: Gold mine; gain 1D8+4 CG If you have a model with the Quartermaster role that was used in, and survived the last game, add an additional +2 CG to any found. 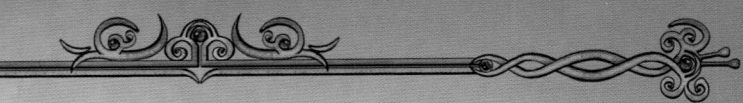
27-28	**Sacred Grove** - Gain 2 Healing Brew equipment items by filling flasks from the holy waters that run through the grove.
31-34	**Village** - Trading gains you either 3 CG or, if instead you have a model with the Mauler role that was used in, and survived the last game, you may randomly select a Rare equipment item by "persuading" the villagers to part with their greatest treasure.
35-36	**Abandoned Hermit's Cave** - Gain 1 CG for some minor supplies left by the previous owner. If you have a model with the Hunter role that was used in, and survived the last game, they find a hidden jewel in a crack in the cave wall – gain an additional 2 CG.
37-38	**A Barren Land** - You find nothing of value in this deserted place.
41-44	**Jousting Lists** - You may enter the local joust and place wagers on the finest horsemen in the realm. For each CG you wager (up to a maximum of 5 CG) you may roll a D8. For each 7 or 8 rolled gain 3D8 CG. But if you roll more 1s than 7s and 8s, you lose all you wagered and a non-GRUNT model of your choice in your Company must roll on the injury table as they try to extricate themselves from the fight amidst allegations of cheating and match fixing!

D88 result	Exploration Result
45-46	**Enemy Messenger** - You encounter an enemy messenger. Roll a die. On a 6+, you capture the messenger. If you have a model with the Master Scout role that was used in, and survived the last game, add +1 to the roll. If you capture the messenger, you gain valuable information about your enemy. In your next Vanguard campaign game, you may add +2 to any dice rolls to choose table sides, choose to be attacker/defender or to go first (any that apply).
47-48	**Thieves in the Night** - You wake to find your food and provisions have been robbed! Lose 2 CG or 2 common items if you do not have enough CG. You need to learn to set a better watch...
51-54	**Market Town** - Trading gains you 2D8 CG and one random Rare equipment item. If you have a model with the Quartermaster role that was used in, and survived the last game, add an additional +1 CG to any gained.
55-56	**Tavern** - You reward your troops with the finest ales in the land at the cost of 2CG. In return, all the models in your Warband you select for your next game, improve their Nerve by 1 until the end of the game (for example, Ne 5+ becomes Ne 4+ for the next game). 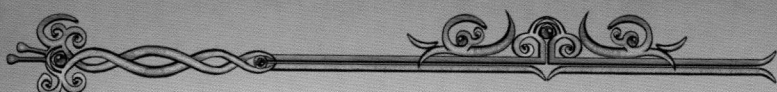
57-58	**Ambush!** - You are attacked by brigands and must make 1 roll each on the Injury table for any 2 non-GRUNT models of your choice in your Company. Companies that have a model with the Master Scout role only make 1 roll on the injury table due to the advanced warning of the attack.
61-64	**Herd of Wild Beasts** - You stumble across plains full of rare wild beasts you can hunt for food and their valuable pelts/hides. Gain 1D8 CG for the pelts/hides. Companies that have a model with the Hunter role instead gain 2D8 from the pelts/hides.
65-66	**The Fighting Pits** - You may enter your strongest troops into the fighting pits to bet on if you are brave enough to take the risk. A single SUPPORT or LARGE non-COMMAND model from your Company can enter the Fighting Pits if you wish. Roll a D8 for each attack the model has. For each 7 or 8 rolled gain 2D8 CG. If you roll more 1s than 7s and 8s, the model cannot be selected in your next Vanguard game while it recovers from its wounds. If a model with the Mauler role is selected as the model to fight, gain an additional 1CG.
67-68	**Refugees** - The fleeing populace have nothing to give and little to steal.
71-74	**Corral** - You are able to find a few mounts running wild that haven't already been captured by other Warbands. You gain a common Mount equipment item. If your model with the Hunter role that was used in, and survived the last game, you may gain a Rare Mount equipment item instead.
75-76	**Nest of Vipers** - You find and eat the rare but dangerous creatures. As an additional bonus you can use their venom to coat your blades. In your next Vanguard game you may give up to 3 models in your Warband the Vicious special rule until the end of the game.

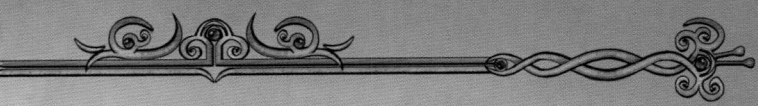

D88 result	Exploration Result
77-78	Wizard's Tower - The old books of lore are worth a lot of money to the right people. Gain 2D8 CG. If your Company has a model with the Arcanist role you may try and learn a new spell from the books you find. Make a Nerve test for the model with the Arcanist role with a -1 modifier. If the test is passed, choose a spell that the model s entitled to learn and add it to the model's profile for free.
81-84	Merchant train - Trading or stealing from the merchant gains your retinue 1D8+4 CG. In addition, if the natural die result is a 5 or more, chose one non-GRUNT model in your Company and roll on the Injury table for them due to being wounded by the wealthy Merchant's bodyguards.
85-86	Goblin slaves - The goblin breeding pits are of value for slaves and trade but whether you free them out of pity and the chance of reward, or buy and trade them, they are tricky and cunning beings. Roll a die. 1-2: the goblins and their masters rob you blind! Lose 4 CG. 3-5: they really are just useless rabble and not worth anything to you. 6-8: some ruthless trading gains you 5 CG. If you have a model with the Quartermaster or Mauler role that was used in, and survived the last game, add an additional +1 CG.
87-88	Dragon's lair - You can choose to explore the Dragon's lair or not! If you choose not to explore you gain nothing, sneaking quietly passed the eerie cave entrance. If you choose to explore roll a die: 1-2: the dragon lives and is furious at being disturbed! Permanently remove a random non-GRUNT model from your warband! 3-5: the lair is abandoned and has been previously ransacked. You gain nothing. 6-7: you find a small treasure hoard gain 1D8+1 CG 8: The dragon is out hunting and you find an unguarded vast treasure hoard. Gain 4D8 CG and a random Unique Item. However, 2 random non-GRUNT models in the company must each roll on the Injury table as they trigger traps in the tunnels left to protect the beast's treasures.

Exploring with Dungeon Saga?

Mantic Games produces the extremely popular fantasy Dungeon Saga board game, set in the same world as both Vanguard and Kings of War. Enterprising and imaginative campaign organisers and gaming groups may wish to take their narrative experience even further and replace some of the results in the table above with games of Dungeon Saga to determine what their warbands and heroes might discover. For example, results such as the Dragon's Lair, Wizard's Tower, Abandoned Mine and Hermit's Cave are all great locations that could be made into a Dungeon Saga adventure.

7. Recruitment and Resupply Phase

At this point, you can spend any unspent CG you have on new equipment or recruits, this is broken down into distinct sections below:

Who shall lead us?

If, at the end of the Exploration phase, a player's Company has no COMMAND models left alive, they must immediately purchase a new one using CG. If they do not have enough CG to purchase another, they immediately gain a COMMAND model (the one with the lowest points value in their faction list) to add to their army, spending as much CG as they have available. Update the unspent CG value on your roster when you are finished. The new COMMAND model is immediately assigned the Leader role. Having to purchase a new COMMAND model to be the Leader in these circumstances doesn't count towards the one model limit on recruiting (see New Recruits below).

Resupply

You may purchase 'Common' equipment and items without restriction. You may only purchase one 'Rare' or 'Unique' item during each Recruitment and Resupply phase, unless the result you rolled during the Exploration Event Table says otherwise. You may only ever own one of each 'Unique' item.

Unwanted items can be sold, netting you half their CG cost (rounding down) as a result. They are then discarded and the amount added to the CG values on the roster.

Drafting Replacements

Any GRUNTS that are killed in a mission are replenished for free each time in the Recruitment & Resupply phase of a campaign game. This must be a like for like replacement with the model that died.

If you wish to replace any other model of a different Class, these must be recruited at normal cost (see below).

New Recruits

You may recruit one new model to your Vanguard Company by spending that model's basic points cost in CG (as detailed on their stat card). Some post-game events may give you an additional 'free' new recruit; this does not count against the one-model limit. All new recruits will start at Rank 0 and with no XP.

As the Recruitment Phase happens after Retinue Assessment, a new recruit will always enter a Company as a basic troop and must earn their stripes in battle if they want to progress.

New Recruits must be taken from your existing faction unless a rule specifies otherwise.

Firing or Retiring company members

Sometimes players may wish to remove a model from their warband, either because they have become a liability or simply to allow them to live out their life basking in the glory (or infamy) they have earnt. Doing so is simple – the model is simply removed from the Roster. Any number of models can be removed in this way during this phase and there is no cost to doing so.

Retinue Roles

If a model with a Retinue role is killed (or chosen to be removed from the Roster), the role may not be assigned to a new recruit until that model has played in at least one game.

8. Confirm Roster Updates

Double-check to make sure you've completed your Company roster. Don't forget to add any increases to your total CG, new Store items, and to note each model's XP, Rank etc.

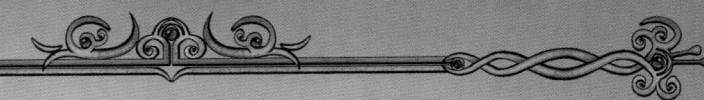

Company Retinue

A Retinue can be as few as only 1 model representing a single Leader role and up to 7 models representing the full set of possible specialist roles.

It is up to each player to decide if they want a large crack team of specialists offering a variety of honed abilities to manage, or a Company with a small Retinue that is supported by a large meat-shield of lesser troops that requires little book-keeping and advancement.

The various roles, with the benefits and restrictions are described in detail here. With the exception of the Healer role, only one of each role may be assigned within a Company.

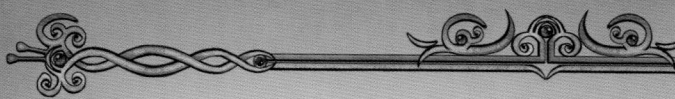

Leader

Restriction: COMMAND models only

Bonus: The model with the Leader role grants an extra Red Power Die when they are used in a game (this free die cannot be upgraded as part of a Rank increase - it is only available for the duration of the game).

Unique role XP: The Leader model gains 1 XP if 3 or more WARRIOR or GRUNT models survive a game the Leader plays in.

Advancement Options: The Leader model may always choose to re-roll on any ability table. At Rank 5, the model with the Leader role has the *Very Inspiring* special rule (if it doesn't already have it). This only applies while the model maintains the Leader Role.

Quartermaster

Restriction: WARRIOR models only

Bonus: If the model with the Quartermaster role plays in a game and survives (wasn't removed as a casualty), add 2 to the "Step 1 – Forage and Loot" roll in the Forage and Explore phase (keep the original dice roll for determining Exploration however). In addition, when any equipment is randomly found, a Company that has the Quartermaster role assigned, may re-roll or re-draw the item that was selected.

Unique role XP: The Quartermaster model gains one extra XP if it survives a game (even if removed as a casualty) and is on the winning side.

Advancement Options: There are no specific rules for this role.

The Arcanist

Restriction: SPELLCASTER models only

Bonus: The Arcanist has the NULLIFY (1) special ability that may be used once per Round. The model with the Arcanist role may attempt to nullify enemy magic. If an enemy SPELLCASTER within 9" of the Arcanist declares they are going to cast a spell, the Arcanist can spend 1 Power to roll 1 die. If the die scores a 5 or more, the enemy spell fails to cast but any action or Power used to make the casting attempt is still used.

Unique role XP: The Arcanist model gains one extra XP if it survives a game (even if removed as a casualty) and cast 5 or more spells.

Advancement Options: At Rank 5, the Arcanist model gains one additional spell. This can be chosen from any spell the Arcanist is eligible to learn.

The Mauler

Restriction: LARGE models only. Must have a Melee stat (not "-")

Bonus: Thump! If the model with the Mauler role causes a wound but doesn't kill its opponent, it may immediately make a second attack against the same target with a single die (before any Retaliations).

Unique role XP: The Mauler model gains one extra XP if it survives a game (even if removed as a casualty) and it caused 6 or more unsaved wounds on enemy models during Melee attacks.

Advancement Options: At Rank 4, the Mauler model may add +1D8 to its Melee attack dice.

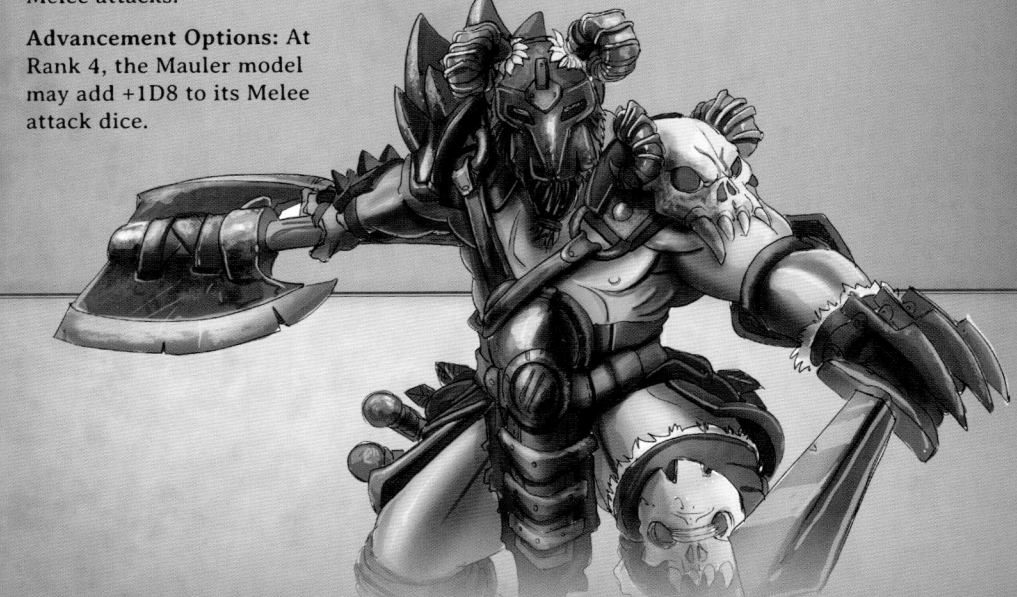

Master Scout

Restriction: Models with the *Scout* rule only

Bonus: In a scenario where the *Scout* rule is permitted, if the model with the Master Scout role is used in the game, after all models are deployed, including those with *Scout*, the Master Scout can be redeployed anywhere on the table using the normal *Scout* rules. If both sides have a Master Scout, roll to see which is moved first.

Unique role XP: The Master Scout model gains one extra XP if it is still in play at the end of the game.

Advancement Options: At Rank 3, the Master Scout may become the Vanguard Bannerman (or woman), responsible for the Company colours. The model gains the *Very Inspiring* rule as its advancement option for this Rank. However, if the Master Scout is killed by an enemy model during a game, the enemy model gets 1 extra XP.

The Healer

Restriction: Any model Class. A Company can have up to 2 Healers.

Bonus: For each model with the Healer role that is used in a game and survives (even if removed as a casualty), you may re-roll any 1 result on the Casualty Table for this or any other model in the Warband after the game.

Unique role XP: None.

Advancement Options: At Rank 3, each Healer grants 1 Bandages equipment item, for free, to its Warband for any game that Healer takes part in. This equipment may be given to any model in the Warband within the normal restrictions.

The Hunter

Restriction: SUPPORT or WARRIOR models only. Must have a Ranged stat (not "-")

Bonus: The model with the Hunter role has the *Pound* special rule on any any ranged attacks it makes.

Unique role XP: The Hunter model gains one extra XP if it survives a game (even if removed as a casualty) and its side killed 3 or more enemy models with ranged attacks (not spells).

Advancement Options: The Hunter model automatically gains the *Marksman* rule if it doesn't already have it. If added because of the role, this CAN be lost if the model is demoted from the role later. At Rank 4, the Hunter model may take a second Ranged stat boost as its advancement (to a maximum of 3+).

COMBINING VANGUARD AND KINGS OF WAR

As well as playing campaigns featuring games purely of Vanguard, a richer and more involved experience can be achieved by combining your games of Vanguard and Kings of War – creating stories of, and between, the larger conflicts. It gives players and gaming groups the chance to create epic narratives, writing the legends from both the daring actions of the plucky few, and the heroic clashes that such missions enable, all played out on the chaotic battlefields of Mantica as empires vie for domination, or simply survival.

Integrating the games and developing such a narrative is usually best organised by a single person – the campaign organiser. They will be the one scheduling and recording games and keeping track of opponents and results. While every gaming group and experienced campaign organiser will have their own way of doing things (some very simple and some downright extravagant!), there are a few simple guidelines to consider when planning a campaign featuring both games.

Of course, each player's KoW army and Vanguard Company/warband must be of the same faction. So if a player is using an Orc army in Kings of War, they will use an Orc faction in Vanguard.

Linked games or not linked games?

Not all games have to be linked. You may want players to engage in a series of Vanguard scenarios to get the campaign started or introduce one-off games at various points in a campaign as Warbands go off in search of adventure and experience. It should be clear to players whether any game of Vanguard they play is going to potentially affect their next game of Kings of War against that same opponent or whether it's an independent scenario.

Narrative

If you have a particular story arc you want players to follow, you may want to dictate which scenarios players use for their Vanguard and King of War games, using either the ones in this book or ones you have made yourself. For example, you may decide that 2 players should play a Light the Beacon scenario for Vanguard followed by a Pillage! KoW game.

How many linked games?

It's recommended that you link no more than two Vanguard games to a following KoW game. Otherwise, too many of the "hooks" and advantages (or disadvantages) would get carried into the KoW battle and become impractical or unfair. Thus, a maximum of two "hook" results from Vanguard scenarios can be used by a player in their next game.

How long do the Vanguard bonuses last for?

Any bonuses or results from the Vanguard scenario "hooks" only apply to the next KoW game against that same opponent (and their same army faction). This should be the next game both players participate in. This logically ties the games together from a narrative point of view and means it doesn't get confusing carrying results around from different games into different match-ups. For example, Sarah and John play a game of Vanguard using their Undead and Goblin Warbands. They then apply any result to their immediate next game of KoW using their Undead and Goblin armies.

Vanguard Campaign-Company Roster

Name		Alignment
		Faction
Campaign Gold	TOTAL	Supplies Caravan
	UNSPENT	
Notes		

Name	Type	Class	Retinue Role	XP	Rank	Points	Injuries

Sp	Me	Ra	Ar	Ne	Wn	Ranged Dice	Melee Dice	Power Dice	Rules & equipment

Name	Type	Class	Retinue Role	XP	Rank	Points	Injuries

Sp	Me	Ra	Ar	Ne	Wn	Ranged Dice	Melee Dice	Power Dice	Rules & equipment

Name	Type	Class	Retinue Role	XP	Rank	Points	Injuries

Sp	Me	Ra	Ar	Ne	Wn	Ranged Dice	Melee Dice	Power Dice	Rules & equipment

Character Record (×4)

Name				Type		Class	Retinue Role	XP	Rank	Points	Injuries
Sp	Me	Ra	Ar	Ne	Wn	Ranged Dice	Melee Dice	Power Dice			Rules & equipment

Name				Type		Class	Retinue Role	XP	Rank	Points	Injuries
Sp	Me	Ra	Ar	Ne	Wn	Ranged Dice	Melee Dice	Power Dice			Rules & equipment

Name				Type		Class	Retinue Role	XP	Rank	Points	Injuries
Sp	Me	Ra	Ar	Ne	Wn	Ranged Dice	Melee Dice	Power Dice			Rules & equipment

Name				Type		Class	Retinue Role	XP	Rank	Points	Injuries
Sp	Me	Ra	Ar	Ne	Wn	Ranged Dice	Melee Dice	Power Dice			Rules & equipment

SUMMARY SHEET

Game Sequence (pg 13)

1. Set up
2. Deploy your models
3. Determine who takes the first turn
4. Play Rounds:
   - a. Roll for Power
   - b. Take alternating Turns
   - c. End Phase
5. Determine the winner!

Power (pg 15 & 20)

Roll at the start of the Round. 3 red dice plus those granted by models. One die can be re-rolled per COMMAND model you have in play.

Power Cost	Purchase
1	+1 model activation
1	+1 dice
1	Forced Fatigue Action
1	Clear Fatigue
2	Group Defence
2	Group Shoot
2	Group Assault
(n)	Model/Warband Special Ability (n)

Engaged (pg 17-18)

Models in base-to-base contact with a standing enemy model are Engaged by it. When a model moves to Engage another model, place the front of the moving model's base flush against the target's base on the side contact was made, as centrally as possible.

- A model that is Knocked-down cannot Engage an enemy model (but can be Engaged by one).
- A standing model that is Engaged by an enemy model can only make *Melee* or *Break Away* actions.

Knocked-down (pg 23)

Any attacks against a model that is Knocked-down are considered to be from its rear arc.

Standard Actions (pg 16-18)

Walk (short) – up to the model's Sp

Shoot (short) – must have a Ranged weapon

Stand Up (short) – Knocked-down models must first stand up

Melee (short) – attack an Engaged model

Cast (variable) – used to cast a spell

Run (long) – up to twice the model's Sp. May qualify as a Charge action (free Melee action)

The *Run* will qualify as a *Charge* action instead if:

1. The moving model had Line of Sight to the Engaged enemy model before it moved AND

2. It took the most direct route it could to the target, only deviating from a straight line to avoid Impassable Terrain or friendly models. In addition, the moving model cannot come within 1" of enemy models it is not going to Engage unless they themselves would be within 1" of the moving model's final position once Engaged.

If the move qualifies as a *Charge* action, the charging model gets an immediate free *Melee* action against the Engaged target.

Brace (long) – improve Ar by 1

Break Away (long) – make an Armour roll (2 escaping a LARGE model). Surviving model may *Run* away from the model they are Engaged with.

Fatigue (pg 19)

During its activation, a model can be given an additional short action. This extra action must be taken after the model's "normal" actions for the Turn. It is known as a Fatigue Action, and the model is then marked as both Activated and Fatigued at the end of its activation. It cannot be a repeat of an action the model already made this Turn (this includes any free *Melee* action as a result of a *Charge*).

A Fatigue Action can also be given to a model that has already activated by spending. This is known as "Forced Fatigue".

A model that is Knocked-down and is lying on the ground must *Stand Up* before it can take any other actions.

FRONT ARC

REAR ARC

Ranged Attacks (pg 27-28)

Modifiers to hit target

- Clear LOS to target = one bonus die
- Shooter on terrain and Height is 3 or more Height levels than target = +1 modifier.

Modifiers to Armour roll

- Shooter's base wholly in rear arc of target = attack gains *Piercing (1)*. Remember, if target is Knocked-down, attack is considered to be from the rear arc.

Target has zero or less wounds?

- If target is a GRUNT, it is removed
- Otherwise, Nerve test with remaining wounds as a modifier.
  - Pass = model remains on 1 wound, is Fatigued and Knocked-down.
  - Fail = removed

Nerve Tests (pg 33)

If the rules say a model must make a Nerve test, roll a single die, applying any modifiers given. If the result is equal or better than the model's Nerve stat, the test is passed. If it is under the models' Nerve stat, the test is failed.

Warband Morale

A Warband is broken if it has less than half the number of starting models remaining. Check at the start of each Round.

Once a Warband is broken, each unengaged model in the Warband must make a Fallback Check the first time it activates in a Round. To make a Fallback Check, simply make a Nerve test:

- If the test is passed, the Fallback Check is successful and the model (or group) may be activated as normal.

If the test is failed, the Fallback Check is not successful and the model (or group) must make a special *Fallback!* action this Turn towards its own table edge (at twice the model's Sp).

Melee Attacks (pg 29-31)

Modifiers to hit target

- Qualifying *Charge* = one bonus die unless enemy defending obstacle or moved through obstacle/difficult terrain
- Target is Knocked-down = +1 modifier
- Outnumbering = 1 bonus die

Modifiers to Armour roll

- Attacker's base wholly in rear arc of target when moving = attack gains *Crushing Strength (1)*. Remember, if target is Knocked-down, attack is considered to be from the rear arc
- Defender behind obstacle and attack in its front arc = Ar improved by 1

Target has zero or less wounds?

- If target is a GRUNT or it is already Knocked-down, it is removed
- Otherwise, Nerve test with remaining wounds as a modifier.
  - Pass = model remains on 1 wound, is Fatigued and Knocked-down.
  - Fail = removed

Follow-up moves

- If a model kills its enemy and there are no other enemy models in base-to-base contact with it, it may make a free follow-up move of 3" into its front arc, following the normal movement rules.

Retaliate

Unless Knocked-down, or both Activated and Fatigued, a model that has been attacked in a Melee and has survived may now Retaliate. Turn to face the model to attack and resolve as normal. Now use the first of the following to apply:

1. If the retaliating model is not already marked as Fatigued, mark it as such with a Fatigued counter.

2. If the retaliating model has not already been marked as Activated this round mark it as such with an Activation counter.

The End Phase (pg 15)

1. Resolve all effects and abilities that take place in the End Phase.

2. Spend any remaining Power to clear Fatigue counters from models.

3. Remove all activation counters and any other counters that are no longer required.

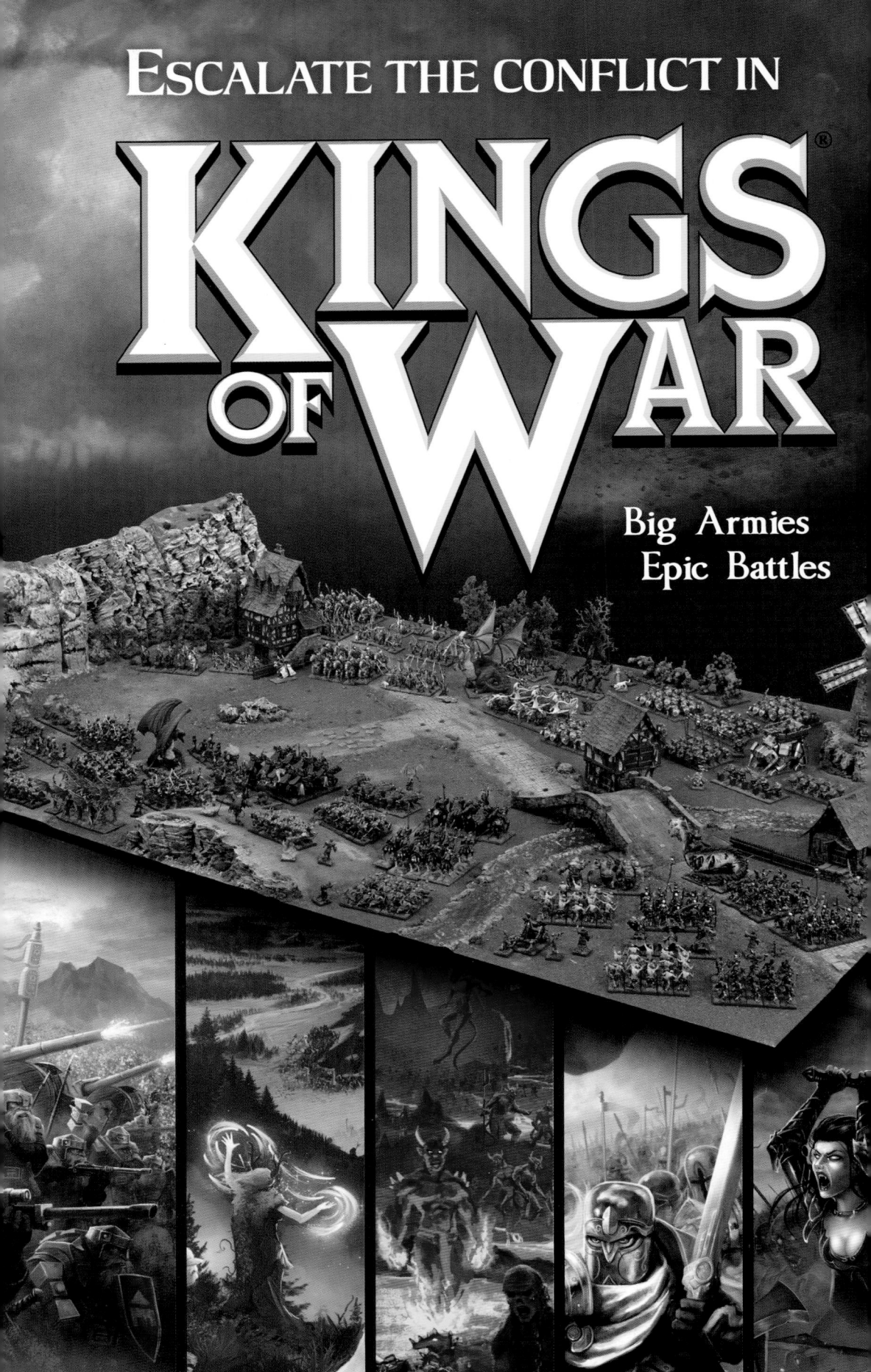

ESCALATE THE CONFLICT IN

KINGS
OF WAR

Big Armies
Epic Battles